Devon's Spiritual Places

The search for God in an ancient landscape

C000020837

A spectacular sky
over Torbay

MOUNGA MOLISI

Devon's Spiritual Places

The search for God in an ancient landscape

Nick Pannell

Contents

First published in Great Britain in 2016

Copyright © Nick Pannell 2016

The moral rights of the author have been asserted.

Published by Blackstone Publications, 179 Marldon Road, Paignton TQ3 3NB

Cover design and formatting: Short Run Press, Exeter, Devon

British Library Cataloguing in Publication Data
A CIP record for this book is available from the British Library

ISBN: 978-1-5262-0470-7

Health, safety and responsibility: This is not a guide book. The author and publisher will not be held
legally responsible for any accident, injury, loss or inconvenience sustained as a result of information
contained in this book. Not all sites featured have full public access. In some cases
permission must be sought from the landowner.

Printed by Short Run Press Ltd, Exeter, Devon

About the author

Nick was born and brought up in Plymouth. He studied at Leeds University before returning to Devon to work as a journalist in Torbay. He was editor of the *Weekender* newspaper and subsequently features editor of the *Herald Express*. He continues to write the popular Bygones feature for the paper. He is author of *Tor Bay: The history and wildlife of Torbay's dramatic shoreline*. He lives in Paignton with his family

Acknowledgements

I am greatly indebted to friends and family who have encouraged this project from its inception. My thanks to Mike Smith, Rachel Nicholson, Paul James, Jon-Paul Hedge and Andrew and Christopher Pannell who have suggested places to visit, contributed photographs and spent long hours reading drafts to improve them. I am grateful to the photographers who have let me use their stunning images as illustrations either for free or small donations. The inferior photographs are my own. I have been reliant on authors of many other books about Devon for much of the background information and forgive me for not referencing fully when they deserve to be. Finally my thanks to the team at Short Run Press for bringing this project to fruition.

Standing stone at Merrivale with Great Mis Tor in the background

Berry Head in June

Introduction

DEVON is a lovely place to live. If you want leisure parks, restaurants, shops and sun-kissed beaches you'll never be short of fun. But if, like me, you think there is more to life and there is a spiritual dimension, then Devon is also a great place to discover it.

Dramatic bronze age monuments give us an insight into the spiritual life of our pre-historic ancestors. We have a wealth of Christian sites, from lonely chapels to towering cathedrals, expressing 2,000 years of faith.

There is also Devon's natural beauty. I have travelled the world but always love coming home to this crumpled-rug of a county with its rich weave of fields, woods, moors and coastline, stitched with rivers and hedgerows.

The French Christian mystic Simone Weil said beauty is often the only way that God can connect with us. "The soul's natural inclination to love beauty is the trap God most frequently uses to win it and open it to the breath from on high".

Each of these 18 chapters will speak to you in different ways. Some are expressions of my own Christian faith, others are simple celebrations of God's creation. It's a geographical journey from storm-lashed Hartland Point to the gentle creeks of South Devon – from moor to sea. The book follows the

unfolding seasons, the colour-mix which makes no visit to a favourite landmark ever the same.

The vast majority of these locations have full public access but please check before you set off. Some are easy to reach, others require an adventurous spirit and preparation, which is appropriate because the spiritual journey is itself an adventure – the most rewarding you can ever make. Of course, what has been a spiritual place for me may not resonate for you. Connecting, sensing His presence, depends on our readiness for new experiences and our longing for His company. He is very close. You don't have to go far. Encounters can be as easily inspired by the rays of a street lamp piercing the gloom on a wet November night as under the arch of the Milky Way on a remote Dartmoor tor.

The poet and Anglican priest R S Thomas wrote of a bright field, "the one field with the treasure in it" – glimpsed once but never forgotten. These are my glimpses, places which have stirred sublime thoughts and assured me we are here for a purpose and not just a cosmic accident. I hope these spiritual places are inspirational for you too and open up a universe of new possibilities and journeys to travel.

Nick Pannell
2016

Voice on the shore

Long Beach, nr Kingswear

The no man's land between cliff top and the low-tide mark offers explorers the most dramatic and challenging landscape Devon has to offer. While the moors can be remote and exhausting, the real drama is where land meets sea.

Here the full force of nature is unleashed: gnawing out sea caves, chiselling pillars of stone, flinging boulders the size of small cars around the bare-rock beach. No visit is the same. The forces which carve these rugged shores never rest; we trespass in a war zone. Because these wild coastlines are difficult to reach, often requiring a scramble over rocks at low tide, they are lonely places.

The falling tide opens a gate to secret coves, deep-cut gullies of kelp and pools, shingle skerries freshly sifted by the retreating sea. The threat of being cut off as the tide turns deters casual visitors.

If you are seeking solitude in a beautiful place, the wild shore is where you'll find it.

My favourite stretch is the low-tide walk between Scabbacombe and Mansands. Access is down a landslip that is always on the move. There is no path because the ground does not remain stable long enough for human feet to shape one. Each descent requires a good stick and creative footwork until you finally reach the solid beach below. Ahead lies a mile of fascinating coast, initially of shingle banked up against the crumbling cliff but soon giving way to more challenging terrain.

There is something mesmerising about a running sea. It conforms to a pattern yet no sequence is the same. It is chaotic but ordered, likely to splash but not engulf. On land there are obvious horizons – a hill-top or church spire – but standing on a beach looking out to sea there is nowhere to focus, just a hazy line which merges with the sky. Distance makes no

"Between the rock and the deep lies the garden, which as the tide falls peeps out as if from under a blanket to reveal its soft face."

sense; the only focus is the endless pulse of waves coming from somewhere beyond the horizon.

Beneath my boots quartz pebbles shift and grind with every step. The tide has thrown up threshed kelp and bladder wrack but this is not a place to stare at your feet. I watch the middle distance where the swell begins to climb and foam, then search beyond. Sometimes there is a ship or pleasure craft but today there is only the infinite sea, curving away over the back of the world.

In ancient times man stood on shores like this wondering what lay out there, seeking knowledge beyond the treacherous rocks and breakers. Then came voyages of discovery, maps, satellites and Google Earth. Now we gaze at the stars and ask the same questions, the horizon lifted just a little.

Today on this wind-lashed shore with the cliffs rising dramatically behind me, gazing out over hundreds of miles of ocean without a ship in sight, I may as well be standing on the edge of the universe.

The wind thumps the sea, sending a chariot of spray across the bay, a breaker grinds another layer off the bedrock, while sediments collect in deep pools to become the mud that will become the shale of a new cliff face to rise up on the other side of the world in future millennia.

And will there be another like me, wandering there before the ocean's vastness, asking the same questions? Maybe his world will have discovered what happened before the Big Bang, measured the heat at the heart of a supernova, counted the stars in the most distant galaxy. But will he yearn, as I yearn, for the purpose?

I sit on the shingle and build a column of quartz pebbles. Within reach there are blue-pearled mussel shells, limpet and clams of intricate shapes. I lay them out in a pattern so they please the eye. The tide has uncovered a pool and I watch snake-lock anemones swirl within it. There is handiwork here.

Far out the rocks are frilled with colourful seaweeds and I watch a flock of oyster catchers race the charging waves into the foam flecked shallows until they see me and swerve away shrieking with alarm. And my mind turns to the Creator who broke the silence of the cliffs, lit the dark water and filled the fathoms with life.

Between the rock and the deep lies the garden, which as the tide falls peeps out as if from under a blanket to reveal its soft face. A bed of kelp sheltering sponges, corals and sea squirts surges with the swell just like breezes ruffle the canopy of trees. Beneath it tiny fish are in their nurseries waiting for their chance in the wide, deep ocean beyond. Delicate it may seem, but life here is as resilient as a limpet's grip on granite.

I return each spring, and despite a winter of rock and sea in brutal conflict the garden lives, not as a bruised survivor but as a returning prince, banners streaming.

Today the cliff and rock echo to the crash of the sea and a deeper boom sounds from the depth of a sea cave as the battle rages at the foundations of the land. I watch a cresting wave catch the hulk of a floating tree and throw it against the rocks like a medieval battering ram.

But the voice I seek is in the garden, a quiet voice, the voice of the gardener.

"In ancient times man stood on shores like this wondering what lay out there, seeking knowledge beyond the treacherous rocks and breakers."

CHRIS MARSHALL

Cathedral in granite

Merrivale, nr Princetown

ANDY STYLES

I am sitting on Dartmoor's Great Mis Tor, tucked amongst granite pillars to escape a brisk March wind. Below is a valley of old fields and walls long abandoned by medieval farmers. The moor has stolen back the land on which they broke their backs, and heather and gorse run riot.

But not everywhere. Amidst the browns and greys of late winter, sheep are grazing on a patch of bright grass elevated above the rough ground. Here, uniform against the chaos, is a stone circle.

Dartmoor walkers will be familiar with Bronze Age settlements. Hillsides are dotted with the remains of the round houses in which our ancestors settled 4,000 years ago as they gathered together in Britain's first stable communities. As I gaze over the valley, my eye discerns other patterns and I realise that this first hut circle is one of many. Around them, an enclosure like a protective parent, draws them together.

I set off down the hillside, the sprung turf boosting every stride. The enclosure wall is easy to climb since the hands of many winters have torn it apart. It now lies in a trailing heap, but I feel safer within. There is reassurance in its embrace.

I wander among circles within circles, find an entrance, then cross an ancient threshold into a hollow that somebody once called home . A course of granite stones still offers protection from the elements, and I unpack and settle in behind them, briefly reclaiming the long-abandoned shelter.

The wind hisses through the grass, switching this way and that like a wild horse. But winter's grip is loosening and the air is full of skylarks and meadow pippets competing for territories with wheatears newly arrived from African shores. How acutely our ancestors must have felt the pulse of the

"A crazy course through the flood-tossed boulders where waterfalls decant into green pools"

5

"To the south a solitary standing stone, over three metres tall, holds vigil"

seasons. On days like this they stepped out and breathed the hope of spring.

In my mind's eye I follow one of these first farmers, as he looks out across the valley and sees his fields and livestock and worries whether wolves have come in the night. Neolithic man did not walk in the footsteps of others or retrace familiar grooves. He was the first to stand amongst the chaos of famine, flood and drought and try to make sense of it. There was one certainty: at the end of the day the sun would set along the western horizon stretched between the rugged peaks of Cox, Stapleton and Roos tors. Along its notches and pinnacles our farmer could trace the passage of the year, a firm fix in a world in flux.

The day draws on and I leave the old village, crossing once more the enclosure wall to the open moorland beyond. Tinners have cut deep into the valley side, and to avoid the gorge I drop down to the stream as the shadows lengthen.

My mind is full of patterns. Strewn granite conjures new circles. Is this a carved stone placed precisely or a random rock? I try to decode the boulder field in the same way a weary traveller gazes upon the landscape of his life, trying to make sense of its peaks and valleys. Is there a path to follow, a way-marked route through the tangled lanes?

I'm by the stream now, following its crazy course through the flood-tossed boulders where waterfalls decant into dark green pools and reeds and mosses crowd in. Then it veers away from the path I want to follow and I head up the hillside again following an ancient instinct for the higher ground.

Then I find them. The hill flattens to a wide plain, and dominating the landscape are two stone rows running for hundreds of yards towards the west. Long winters have battered this sacred avenue – some of the stones now barely break the turf – but the expression survives. Burial cairns nearby suggest it was a special place to be interred, while to the south a solitary standing stone, over three metres tall, holds vigil. Here man was inspired to build and shape, finding time beyond the drudgery of his daily life to express in simple granite forms sublime and lofty thoughts. It was worth doing because there was something to say. It was worth saying because others needed to know.

To know what? I follow the avenue in silence. The wind has dropped as the sun has lost its strength, and birds are mute. Only ravens speak on a distant tor.

> *"Neolithic man did not walk in the footsteps of others or retrace familiar grooves. He was the first to stand amongst the chaos of famine, flood and drought and try to make sense of it."*

Even now, 4,000 years on, there is comfort in the order and geometry of the stones on a moorland where there is little of either. As I walk the plain I find others – menhirs, cists and cairns laid out before the setting sun in a sacred landscape charged with meaning. How successive generations must have come, as I have come and been inspired. Here was Devon's first cathedral, inarticulate stone raised up to frame and prompt a conversation with a power beyond.

My day ends in the centre of a stone circle watching the sun set behind the jagged ridge of the Staple Tors and for a moment we are united, me and the Neolithic farmer. My thoughts race in the footprints of his reaching out to our Creator.

ROSS HODDINOTT

Breaking news from a lofty pulpit

Brentor, nr Tavistock

No map is needed. Brentor Church stands above the rolling hills of west Devon as a pinnacle visible for miles around. It may be one of the smallest churches in the county, but it towers above all others.

It has stood as a beacon of the Christian faith for nearly 1,000 years, proclaiming a message as deeply rooted as the volcanic core on which it stands.

I've entered Plymouth Sound in a small boat, seen its distinct profile to the north and felt assured of firmer ground. After a day of heavy rain and mist, I've glimpsed its silhouette in the rays of a late sun and sensed the promise of better days to come. Since childhood it has drawn my gaze.

It's April, and the road from Tavistock is ablaze with beech trees. I reach a small car park then follow a steep, grassy track, passing flowering hawthorn and occasional clumps of bluebells until the path becomes a flight of steps to a church gate.

All around are views of deepest Devon bordering an even remoter Cornwall; only the busy A30 connects this ancient landscape to the modern world. Far below, cattle are lumbering through a field toward a dew pond, unhurried but purposeful in their search for water. From a small copse I can hear the chatter of rooks, and beyond them the open moors,

"All around are views of deepest Devon"

still barren after a long winter, though a hint of green suggests the bracken is at last breaking through the leaf litter to reclaim the land.

I arrive at the church like a bridegroom full of expectation. Small it may be, but everything is here – a tiny churchyard, porch and tower sheltering a cosy, intimate interior. Windows set deep into the granite walls illuminate two rows of six pews. I sit down, unloading my rucksack onto the polished oak. It is a significant act. Tourists walk around Devon's great churches by the coach load but rarely sit. To sit is to engage, to sit is to connect with the purpose of the place and risk an encounter with the divine, or not. To sit is to become vulnerable to the possibility that having travelled all this way there may be nothing to discover on this incongruous crag save the stones of an old building.

The wind whistles around the eaves and the first drops of an April shower pelt the windows. The church darkens, a draught stirs the air and there is a faint smell of a failing damp course and mouldering books. So many books. They've changed the Bibles and hymnals but not taken the old ones away, and they are stacked in a corner like loose bricks.

I'm hungry for inspiration. The parishioners who built this church weren't short of it. Over how many years did they hurry up the hillside dressing the stone, building the walls, setting the roof to withstand the worst of weather to create this sanctuary to God? Faith was surging and the ruined hill fort, built by their pagan forebears, was stripped of stone and put to new use. Now they trusted in God and resurrection and proclaimed their hope from the hilltop.

But here on this intemperate Spring day with the hymn rack empty and dying flowers by the altar, I'm ambushed by thoughts as insistent as the gusts of wind outside. Perhaps the builders got it wrong and the rock of faith is flawed. Perhaps Brentor's destiny is a museum to a misplaced hope, not the beacon of an active one.

I open a Bible. This one book has seeded a million others as man has tried to make sense of that Easter morning when the compass spun and the first believers rushed to their neighbours with breaking news. So many words, yet those on the lips of the pioneers were simple ones. A man had been raised from the dead, they said, and everything had changed.

The Bible on my lap is open at the Book of Psalms. I read eagerly like a scientist poring over data, searching for

the spark of light that can unlock a whole new universe of understanding. Yet the words, like the stone, echo back empty, without resonance, music or meaning.

I drift into stories my father once told me, the Brentor of lay lines, hidden treasure, giants, Devils and shipwrecked sailors. Myths and legends swirl around this church like Dartmoor mist until all is obscured. Is there anything to be found here? And yet the page is still open, and with rain now lashing the church there is no point in leaving. Sit tight old traveller.

Then words begin to glow. Psalm 46: "Be still and know that I am God". The simplicity grabs me, freeing me of the vast libraries of modern religious thought and theology, its debates and contradictions, its fussy rituals and ornate cathedrals onto the bare rock of faith.

"Be still" says God, and know that I am with you.

At its simplest, Brentor says just that. The hands of men wielding brick and barrow have given shape and substance to a 2,000-year-old revelation, the breaking news passed on to others through a lofty pulpit that is never silent. "I am" says God from the top of this old volcano, "Come and explore".

Sacred groves

Bridge Woods, nr Chumleigh

To the north of the moors, around the Taw and its tributaries, lie the sacred groves of Devon. Two thousand years ago a Celtic people lived in these deep, wild woods and they worshipped the nature which governed their lives. Sun and moon were Gods, rivers and streams were sacred and among the mighty oaks they created places for ritual worship.

The coming of Christianity in the 2nd century AD displaced pagan belief, but the Celtic saints did not lose a reverence for nature. They sensed in the same remote woods a divine presence – a pulse that beat beyond the life of trees – that inspired and enthralled them. So sacred they remained, and the memory of them is preserved in place names hereabouts. Villages and hamlets carry various derivatives of the Celtic word 'nemeto' or 'nemitis', meaning sacred grove. There are more than a dozen Nymets, Nympton and Nymphs in this corner of Devon, a link to a time when God was found in the midst of nature, not confined within the walls of churches.

I'm at the entrance to Bridge Woods near Chumleigh, a ribbon of ancient woodland in a fold of hills. Such woods once covered the county, but 4,000 years of farming have left only remnants – often in steep valleys which no ploughs can reach. It's a remote oasis, the footpath to its gate little worn, and as I cross its threshold I leave the bright fields and distant views for another room in the glorious mansion of May.

Here all is green, towering and enveloping, filling the senses with different smells and sounds to those of the open meadow. I'm greeted by a swath of bluebells fringed by a border of campions, stichwort and herb Robert. A hazy sun is still able to reach the forest floor through a filter of infant leaves where an understorey of hazel, ferns and holly makes the most of it before the canopy closes shut.

Birdsong is intense, the contours of the valley amplifying the peeps and shrilling of hidden songsters. Nature is at its

"Here I take my seat at the festival of Spring, the symphony of colour at full volume, abundant flora like the instruments of an orchestra adding their own chord to the harmony."

most effusive and audacious, but, like stepping into someone else's party, my presence disturbs it. From the branches above me, woodpigeons take fright, their wings clapping wildly, which scares a squirrel. Then further away I hear something bigger, probably a deer, hastening through undergrowth away from me.

In my childhood I was frightened of woods. They were dark, mysterious places where children in fairy tales got lost and came to bad ends. But as I grew and spent time in the wildest of them they became like walled gardens, safe and protected. It was the world beyond that seemed threatening and out of control.

The path leads slowly downhill, the sound of the stream in the valley growing louder as I approach, then I leave the trail for a dappled glade where the roots of a 200-year-old oak tree have created a cosy niche. Here I take my seat at the festival of

Spring, the symphony of colour at full volume, abundant flora like the instruments of an orchestra adding their own chord to the harmony.

At my feet is a jungle – fresh, keen growth in a race for life. To observe just a yard of this savannah is wonder enough. But my eye is enticed down corridors of trees to sunlit antechambers, hollows and oriels of the deeper forest, and I sense I'm at the heart of a great cathedral with so much more to explore. Like sunlight through a stained-glass window plays on the patterns of medieval tiles so the May sun dapples the woodland floor through a tracery of leaves. And from the canopy birdsong soothing the fretful mind.

Celtic saints saw in nature the irrepressible self-expression of a joyful, generous God. It is in springtime, in green temples such as this, that His power surges – and beauty too, beyond

"The path leads slowly downhill, the sound of the stream in the valley growing louder as I approach"

the palate of human art. Here, in the bower of Bridge Woods, God feels close.

But this is no heaven. In the foreground stands the shattered trunk of a once-great tree, snapped by a violent gust, its crown splintered and rotting amongst nettles. Tranquillity is of a moment and beauty doomed to fade. There is no hiding place from the gale of life, the changing season or passage of years, not least in the sacred groves of Devon. The crooked worm gorges on at the heart of the oak.

I leave the glade, and rejoin the path to reach the valley bottom where the stream is at last visible, creeping through lush undergrowth over a bed of shale.

I jump down onto a shingle bank thrown up by winter floods, mould a seat from the stones and enjoy lunch while the theatre of nature plays on. Woods engross the senses, so distracting the mind that the cares of the world dissolve. Happily immersed, I wander on – unhurried and slightly lost, through the long afternoon enjoying sylvan therapy in a sacred grove.

Then the spell is broken. Turning a corner a bulldozer violates the space, its rusting bucket jammed into a boulder.

It had been excavating the hillside, leaving a gouge of bare shale, but then abruptly abandoned. Drawing close I can see that nature is already reclaiming it. Brambles have snared its tracks and forced open the engine box. In its cab a silver birch has taken root, a mighty machine of man an anchorage for new life, which will in time consume it.

As beauty is transitory, so is ugliness – nature programmed to seal the scar and renew the sacred forest. In the tender shoots reaching up to gently prise the steel plates apart I sense the tenacity of God to restore Eden.

Refreshed at a sacred spring

Broadclyst holy well, nr Exeter

A long thirsty summer staggers into August. It hasn't rained for weeks and Devon's muddy pasture has become a jigsaw puzzle of hard-fired clay. The only water is in drinking troughs choked with algae, which draw swarms of flies that then pester the cattle which dare approach them. Days are long and fretful, marooned between the flourish of spring and the cleansing storms of autumn.

In the hedges and margins of fields beyond the reach of grazers the flowers are stunted, late-blooming foxgloves shaking a fist of flowers at the sun because they have no energy to stand tall before it.

Trees are ragged, bearing a skin of old leaves which have become taut and brittle. I'm in Broadclyst, and, like the whole of nature it seems, searching for refreshment.

"Devon's complex landscape of lanes, footpaths, copses and coombes hides its secrets"

"Algae and ferns glow luminous in the shadows, creating strange patterns on surrounding walls"

I'm looking for a holy well, but Devon's complex landscape of lanes, footpaths, copses and coombes hides its secrets. "*A dilapidated gate leads into a wood about quarter of a mile down the B road*" read my instructions, but there are many gates and small woods and I'm standing here hot and bothered not knowing which way to turn.

I approach the fringe of a small copse that looks promising and push through a curtain of vegetation into a tunnel of green, sunlight snared and diminished by the smothering trees. It's a relief to be out of the sun, but there is little comfort here in an understorey of nettles and brambles.

I was hoping to pick up a path to the well but instead I'm struggling through a dense thicket of hawthorn, hazel and ash, which hasn't been breached in years. I pause as a traveller who has lost his way pauses, not knowing whether to continue or retrace his steps.

The fierce heat of the open fields has given way to a cage of trunks and branches. The air reeks of fermenting leaf mould as the forest feasts on its own decay. Here too, the land is thirsty but even deeper so.

I press on, encouraged by a glimpse of alder, a familiar sight along the river courses of Devon because of its love of water, and I'm quickly rewarded. Here, in a cradle of green, is the Broadclyst holy well.

Little is known of its origins. It's setting is remote and if it wasn't for its ornate housing it would have disappeared long ago under moss and marsh. A well house of dressed stone forms an entrance beneath a neat Roman arch. Two cushion capitals descend, creating the impression of a small temple and a mysterious interior. It was built in the early 19th century by Charles Cockerell who built Killerton's Romanesque chapel about a mile away, giving grand status to a traditional sacred spring.

I draw closer. The dry ground gives way to a damp, spongy floor and towering stems of hog weed and cow parsley crowd in. Few pilgrims seek Broadclyst's holy well today, but nature worships here with broad lush leaves.

Inside the well house I can see a basin of cool, clean water accessible down two short steps, but the water that pools here has never been contained by the mason's hands and has spilled out to create a blooming oasis. In the sunlight the pink flowers of campion and herb Robert decorate the stonework while liverwort and hart's tongue fern have found niches in the shadows. The forest of stems are home to hoverflies, speckled wood butterflies and a hundred other creatures feasting at nature's table. On the margins, sloe and elderberry ripen in the sun.

Some people still come seeking the miraculous at Broadclyst's holy well. On branches above it, visitors have tied ribbons which flutter in the wind like prayer flags. But no offerings are needed here; whatever flows is freely given and the miracle is all around.

The water that feeds the root, which nurtures the flower, which seeds the fruit, which feeds the man is the miracle of Eden, and the flourish of life in this woodland glade on this parched August day is no less extraordinary. Every spring should be sacred.

I descend the steps into the well. The 19th century plumbing has long failed, but a modern pipe has been installed to siphon some water elsewhere. Algae and ferns glow luminous in the shadows, creating strange patterns on surrounding walls. The surface is calm but I sense a current moving through it, loosening occasional bubbles which disturb the fringe of moss.

"Whatever flows is freely given and the miracle is all around"

Water. So abundant during most of the year but not this day. It is held and treasured here like a god within its temple. Around me everything is solid, sharp and physical but the pool beneath the Roman arch is wholly other, transcendental, reflecting the vastness of the sky. I touch it with fascination. For a moment it seems to resist my dry, dusty fingers but then embraces them, soothing and flowing this way and that until the surface dances with light.

I return the way I came, back through the hungry wood and baked fields under the same unremitting sun longing for the springs to gush again and quench the land.

BUCKFAST ABBEY

Here might I stay and sing

Buckfast Abbey, Buckfastleigh

Some journeys are worth taking just for the welcoming hug.

I'm on the road from Paignton to Buckfast Abbey, one of Devon's great religious sites, for a rendezvous with a friend whose company I seek above all others.

It's a pretty ride. After Totnes the road follows the course of the Dart as it tumbles down from the moors over weirs and rapids. It's early morning and the crowds which flock to the abbey during the tourist season have yet to arrive. I park easily and stride the gravel path towards the abbey, a magnificent building bathed today in morning sun and on other days I may have stopped, taken a picture or two, and admired the setting. But today I'm not interested in architecture (inspiring though it is) but an engagement I've no wish to delay.

I enter the nave of the abbey church and the hushed solemnity slows my steps. The foundations rest on 1,000 years of history and this is no place to hurry. It took the builders 30 years to resurrect the building in the early years of the 20th century after 500 years of ruin, stone raised on stone with simple block and tackle. There is rhythm to the life of the abbey that defies the pace of modern life, like a back eddy in the swirling flow. Many come to Buckfast Abbey for religious retreats to recover the cadence of a calmer life.

In the spirit of a pilgrim approaching his destination, I descend the nave, the arches and choir stalls framing the high altar. In the side aisles I glimpse the Stations of the Cross, the narrative of Easter, set in Romanesque niches. I know this place, I've been coming since I was 14 years old, and anticipation grows as I reach the transept. Beyond a new light shines and there I see him, arms outreaching, waiting to embrace me. A few more steps and I'm in the Chapel of the Blessed Sacrament before the finest stained-glass depiction of Jesus of Nazareth I know as teacher and friend.

His gaze draws me closer as if he's spotted me in a crowd and has beckoned me nearer. I am now within an intimate circle, dimly lit, seated before him. The only sound is of

"Many come to Buckfast Abbey for religious retreats to recover the cadence of a calmer life."

running water from an interior fountain and I imagine a timeless place, a simple Galilean cave or dwelling, where 2000 years ago he would have sat with his followers talking about the Kingdom of Heaven.

We meet, not in a physical sense but as family, too long separated, reunited with smiles and joy around a table, renewing conversation and companionship. There's a banquet prepared. The Jesus of the Buckfast chapel sits before a table set with bread and wine. There is hospitality here and acceptance, a place already reserved.

Lines from scripture come to mind like half remembered tunes. "Come to me all who are weary . . .", "Let anyone who is thirsty come to me and drink". I recall the Broadclyst holy well, the August heat and the cool water running freely. I drink deeply.

Then I sense the warmest of embraces, a hug more meaningful than any words, enveloping and protective. It is the hug which greeted the Prodigal son on his return to his father's house after years away. The journey is over and a relationship restored. I feel a rucksack of worldly care lifted from my shoulders and I feel safe.

Now the attention of the Jesus of the Chapel of Blessed Sacrament falls solely on me. Sometimes our connection with Him can be like a poor Skype signal, the image wobbles and disappears but here the face of Jesus is steady and assured, the vast 26ft stained-glass window turning daylight into a glowing tapestry of colour. Outside the sun is climbing high above the pinnacles of the abbey tower, bleaching the stone work. Inside the sun's power is melded by the artist's hand through prisms and facets to create the figure of Christ at the sacramental table, in deepest blues and purples.

"I descend the nave, the arches and choir stalls framing the high altar"

"His gaze draws me closer as if he's spotted me in a crowd and has beckoned me nearer. I am now within an intimate circle, dimly lit, seated before Him."

Outside the world hurries on to the next appointment, but here time has stopped – the metronome paused – His presence my only reality as lovers engrossed become oblivious to those around them. Jesus – the Alpha, and the Omega, the beginning and the end – and me together in a Devon chapel in the glow of eternity.

As the hymn writer rejoices:

"Here might I stay and sing,
No story so divine,
Never was love, dear king
Never was grief like thine.
This is my Friend,
In whose sweet praise
I all my days
Could gladly spend"

"Grief like thine?". The words linger, changing the mood like a cloud moving over the sun, and I look again into the face of Christ searching for understanding and in those deep red eyes I feel the conversation moving on, the scene widening. I see too the gaze of the suffering servant, the man of sorrows, betrayed and executed on a barren hilltop far from home and enjoined still in the pain of the world. Jesus shines in the tranquillity of a Devon abbey but he looks too on the bombed city, the torture cell and orphanage. Are those eyes red with tears?

And I sense the intimate circle I have joined growing, new seats occupied. Hands join with mine – rough hands, broken hands, tiny hands – an expanding fellowship across language, creed and colour no building can contain. The small chapel of the Blessed Sacrament now has the atmosphere of an expectant stadium His universal church gathered together beyond the dimensions of any roof. We are all here, with our own experiences of the divine star, drawn by personal invitation and united by his embrace.

Come eat . . . come drink, the banquet is set.

Where quiet waters flow

Halsdon, nr Dolton

There are oases of time when seasons linger, quiet days before the next dramatic act unfolds when nature seems in no great hurry to change the set.

And so I find myself in the valley of the River Torridge at Halsdon, a Devon Wildlife Trust reserve in one of the remotest areas of the county. The forecast is good, although mare's tails scribbled across the sky hint at change to come .

Halsdon covers 142 acres of outstanding habitat along a river celebrated in Henry Williamson's novel Tarka the Otter. It's a place to lose yourself, relax by the water and embrace a warm September sun one last time.

A track from a small car park descends through thick woodland its steep sides a tangle of summer growth. Squirrels are busy in the hazel coppice gathering nuts and a light breeze loosens the first acorns, which drop to the ground with a thud. It's a descent into tranquillity, the trials of the journey through narrow lanes forgotten by the time I reach the river.

Born in the slates and shales of the Culm grassland following a long, slow arc through Devon coombes, how cheerfully it greets me with its flowering banks and sparkling currents. The tumbling brook of the higher reaches has matured into a majestic, silver-haired waterway gliding effortlessly over well-worn stones. The sea beckons, the journey is almost done.

Alder and ash now form a noble avenue along its course and in their shadow I glimpse the ruins of

"How cheerfully it greets me with its flowering banks and sparkling currents"

> *"Here the course of the river is in constant flux, building up and throwing down, creating deep, slow-moving pools, pebble shoals, islands and rapids"*

an old mill and weir where man once tried to harness the power of the river, but it has shaken loose its bonds and now flows unhindered among the scattered stones of our proud engineering. "Men may come and men may go but I go on forever" sings the river in Tennyson's famous poem not mentioning that it will erase our footprints too.

The woods give way to open pasture where the sun is burning off the last of the dew. Rosehips, sloes and blackberries are bulging in the hedgerows – the fruits of a long and manic summer – but the stems that championed them are tired like a worker at the end of his shift. Where Spring floods threw up fresh banks of silt, nature has sown a meadow. The violet and mauve flowers of balsam are blooming still, their sweet aroma carried on light airs along the river bank. In pools of light, insects are nectaring on the last of the flower heads, among them bold, bright red admiral butterflies – flag-bearers of the retreating season. Everywhere nature is gathering harvest before the pantry door swings shut.

I am searching too. I've strolled the woods and followed the river for over a mile, exploring every corner of this gracious valley. Now I want a place to sit and savour the beauty, drink its sights and sounds, let the serenity distil within me, then carry it home as a souvenir. Spiritual places should recharge and inspire us long after we have left.

I cross a stile into part of the reserve that is restricted to visitors in the summer months, but where in late September you can wander freely. The Torridge too has found new expression in a broad flood plain where it meanders through silts and shingles deposited in previous deluges. Here the course of the river is in constant flux, building up and throwing down, creating deep, slow-moving pools, pebble shoals, islands and rapids.

Where the bend of the river is sharpest it has carved inland cliffs where sand martins burrow and nest in spring. At one point the river becomes so wide and shallow I'm tempted to paddle across it. Below this sluice the river decants into a great green pool overhung by trees. It is here, on a swath of grass growing soft and thick atop an old sandbar, that I stop, slip off my bag and relax.

I have known places like this all my life. When I was a child my mother would take me and my brothers onto the moors to swim in secret pools when the beaches were too crowded.

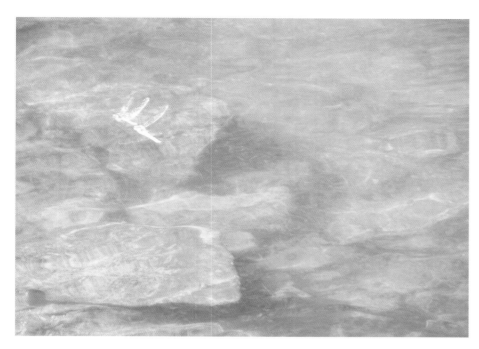

slow relentless pull towards the sea. Then I see my own reflection on the canvas of the pool, pensive and motionless among the last flowers of summer, and the river moving through us.

I shape a pillow of grass, lie back and, immersed in deep and restful thoughts, fall soundly asleep.

"Only occasionally is the mirror disturbed by a rising trout or skipping dragonfly"

They fascinated me. Tiny flows of water pouring into deep lagoons – peat-brown, bath-warm – fringed by bracken and heather. There I paddled and swam over golden, quartzy sand under the watchful eye of my mother. And here I am again, beside still waters, secure still in the knowledge of love, but of a higher order than ever revealed during those infant days.

The pool holds my gaze. Framed within its margins is a perfect reflection of the view around me, a symmetry of bank, tree and sky. Only occasionally is the mirror disturbed by a rising trout or skipping dragonfly and then the ripples spread out and out until the fringes gently rock.

I study the reflection. The image is static and yet I notice the medium is moving imperceptibly beneath it. The flow is slower than a man can walk – it barely moves at all – and yet it is not still. It has irresistible direction which only the tipping of the continent could reverse – the

DAVE DUMMETT

At the mercy of the sea

Hartland Point

I'm standing on a platform of bare rock just feet above a raging Atlantic Ocean, buffeted by gale-force winds and spray. I'm at Hartland, Devon's Cape Horn, a stretch of coast that takes nature's fury on the chin.

Swells, churned in the milieu of the open sea, gaining height and power over 5,000 miles of brooding ocean, are charging at the face of the land. As they approach they arch upwards like spear throwers, before unleashing a volley of white water at the base of the cliff. Each wave is delivered like a punch, seeking out a weakness, while the roaring wind – like a ringside crowd – urges them on to greater strength and menace. On the horizon, spotlights of sun highlight fresh battalions marching landward, the relentless armies of the ocean besieging the land.

We think we've mastered the elements, ordered the anarchy of nature, but standing here before these giant breakers, experiencing the unfettered power of wind and sea, I'm reminded that we haven't. On this tenuous cliff edge, as with our lives, chaos and disaster are at the gates. Destruction is just feet away. As the waves realign the boulders on the beach, reshape the skerries and shoals with each scouring tide, so I rediscover my frailty in a brutal world.

The sea – wild, confused and unpredictable – holds dominion at Hartland. On the south coast of Devon, quaint harbours and sheltered inlets offer ready shelter to mariners – but not here. For unrelenting miles saw-toothed reefs stretch out to seaward, able to pierce the strongest hull. More than 200 wrecks are recorded beneath these cliffs and at low tide mangled metal litters the shore.

But the most potent reminder of the sea's power to trash the ambitions of men lies in the scattered remains of Hartland Quay. This citadel against the Atlantic Ocean was built in

"The sea – wild, confused and unpredictable – holds dominion at Hartland"

29

DAVE DUMMETT

Hartland Quay in the 19th century

the 16th century, and for 300 years provided shelter for sailing smacks and sloops plying their trade between South Wales and North Devon. Behind a 40ft wide quay wall, strengthened by mortar and iron staples, boats could ride out the weather, though the hawsers securing them would strain and buck in the heaving swells. There would be daily dramas as boats carrying limestone, coal and slate would attempt the narrow entrance. Ships were wrecked and lives lost – while the small community in the quayside cottages looked on powerlessly. But behind that wall there was safety from the turmoil that raged beyond it.

Those who depended on the harbour for a living fought desperately to maintain it. In 1841 the pier head had to be rebuilt after it was destroyed in winter gales. A few years later the counter pier was swept away and never replaced. Storms wrecked the pier head again in 1887 and this time there was not enough money to repair it. On October 8 1896 the sea breached the final stronghold – the mole – carrying away three centuries of effort to preserve a sanctuary on this hostile shore. With the loss of the quay went dozens of livelihoods – hopes and plans strewn, like the stones of the pier, at the mercy of the sea.

I retreat from the wave line and make my way back to the cove, where low tide reveals the very last of the foundation stones of Hartland Quay jammed into bedrock. They built wisely, the Elizabethan masons – on the rock as the old parable taught – but it was not enough. Sometimes storms overwhelm all human endeavour and we can only cower before them.

The gale strengthens, the thump of waves intensifies, and with no wish to linger in this scarred and solemn place I hurry up the path to where a more distant perspective lightens my mood. Then the track drops again, not to a storm-lashed shore but to a valley and a stream sheltered by trees. After crossing the bridge, I turn inland to be greeted with an inspiring sight – the 128ft tower of St Nectan's church – like a human arm punched skyward, defying the chaos. Both muscular and elegant, it stands with singular presence in the Hartland landscape, a practical aid to navigation and a symbol of faith at the ocean's edge.

I'm in the valley of St Nectan, a Celtic missionary, who in the 5th century AD braved the wild Atlantic to land here and live out the rest of his life as a hermit. He carried ashore a revelation – a message of hope and a new way of living of such transforming power that 1500 years later his name is still revered. The church of Stoke carries his dedication and his name is linked to other holy sites in the area . But no further; St Nectan is a very local saint.

The gale at my back pushes me up the footpath towards the church, the tower of which grows ever larger as I approach. The door is open and I'm greeted by a warm interior and a friendly face. "Welcome" says the churchwarden, who is preparing for an evening concert and, embraced in a spirit of hospitality, I stroll the aisles soaking up 1,000 years of history.

In a side chapel the story of St Nectan is preserved. A wood carving and painting depict a simple traveller, staff in hand

with the sea at his back. In another corner a tapestry shows an ark being tossed by violent waves and I think again of St Nectan in his little boat, chancing all on the ocean of life, approaching the wild Hartland shore and its ferocious reefs with trepidation, but trusting in God and good seamanship to carry him through. I think of the boat lurching as a breaking wave catches the hull, the crash of white water, the groan of planks – until, by the grace of God, he is carried ashore.

And his work beginning, not as a builder of harbours, but of faith laid in the hearts of men.

"St Nectan's church – like a human arm punched skyward, defying the chaos"

> *"Magnificent stained glass once threw coloured light over white-washed walls, but today it's the fleck of moss and algae clawing at old mortar that lends the colour. All that was delicate, vulnerable and comforting has gone"*

Consumed in the furnace of war

Charles Church, Plymouth

Plymouth city centre was levelled by bombing in 1941 but 70 years later there is barely a reminder of the fire or the death and destruction that raged through the streets. But at the junction of dual carriageways, overlooked by a brash new shopping centre and stranded in a roundabout, is a surviving witness: the shattered remains of Charles Church.

Public access is not encouraged. To reach it requires a dash across lines of moving traffic, and once there entry is denied by chained iron gates. This is not a place for quiet reflection within a sanctuary of noble walls. The ruins provoke questions that take you back to the darkest moments of Plymouth's history and to the door of human suffering.

As a child growing up in Plymouth in the 1960s I stepped lightly here. My parents rarely spoke of the city's blitz, but through overheard conversations and the grim spectacle of remaining bomb sites I learned that something terrible had happened.

Three thousand high-explosive bombs fell and 219,000 incendiaries. 4,500 houses and dozens of public buildings, including 41 churches, were destroyed. 1,172 lives were lost. Horror piled on horror. A direct hit on the city hospital maternity unit killed 19 children and four nurses, and not far from Charles Church, in Portland Square, 72 people died when a bomb burst through the roof of an air-raid shelter. One father was asked to identify the bodies of his wife and five children.

Charles Church, a place of worship since the 17th century, saw it all and was itself consumed by it. On the nights of 21 and 22 March, 1941 the flames of the church joined an inferno of such intensity that the glow could be seen across Devon.

Those who lived through the destruction, who breathed the stench of fire, dug for loved ones in the rubble and grieved beside mass graves (292 civilians were buried in a single plot in Efford Cemetery) spent the next few decades rebuilding their lives and the city. But they preserved this ruin, this gutted church with its smashed altar, for us to contemplate.

I have come in November, a time of year when fresh poppy wreaths lie vivid red against the stone of war memorials across the county. It's late afternoon – the pavements are busy with shoppers and the traffic lanes around Charles Church are choked with cars. For a moment the queues judder to a halt and I am able to dash between stationary lorries to reach the safety of the roundabout. Years of road building have left the old church in a kind of hollow so the traffic rumbles above it, red brake lights flickering across the eastern walls in the winter gloom.

I seek an entrance, but the archways are either bricked up or gated and I end up peering through rusty, spiked railings. The interior arches are preserved, but where ordered pews, pulpit

"Here, preserved in this ugly ruin, is the memory of those darkest days when God seemed trampled too."

and choir stalls once furnished an inspiring 17th century Gothic church there's only grass dissected by rough paths of flattened gravestones.

Magnificent stained glass once threw coloured light over white-washed walls, but today it's the fleck of moss and algae

clawing at old mortar that lends the colour. All that was delicate, vulnerable and comforting has gone, consumed in the furnace of war. Now it's a place of jagged stone open to the weather in a no-man's land of modern development. Even the dead have left, bodies in the old churchyard reinterred elsewhere when the Exeter Road was widened.

And what of God, in whose name this church was built? Did he leave too the night the bombers came, dropping 1000lbs bombs into family living rooms?

"But faith did not perish here."

I run my fingers along the rough granite of an archway and try to connect with the people who stood amongst the ruins on that desperate morning, with smoke still rising from charred timbers, and who looked to God for answers. He must have seemed as powerless as them at the savage hands of men. And I sense the despair that still lurks in the shadows of Charles Church, this Plymouth Calvary where the innocent suffered and death held dominion. Here, preserved in this ugly ruin, is the memory of those darkest days when God seemed trampled too.

But faith did not perish here. The following Sunday the people of Charles Church came together with others who had lost their churches and marched up the hill to the Hoe where they worshipped God as one.

Even before the war had ended, churches were being rebuilt. The nearby Minster of St Andrew's would be fully restored, encouraged by the defiant sign *Resurgam*, meaning "I will rise again", found nailed to the front door the morning after it was burnt down. Kings Street Methodist Church, destroyed the same night as Charles Church, would be rebuilt as would the Salvation Army's Congress Hall in Martin Street.

But there was no resurrection here beneath the cold, granite tower of Charles Church, no dressing the wound to shield the eye. It is left bare and open, like a battlefield, with just enough maintenance to preserve it.

So amidst the brash hoardings, bright lights and blaring cars

of a modern consumer city there's another message, audible to those who might pause and ask 'what do these stones mean'? On a chill November night 70 years on, the words still resonate: "We suffered here".

NIGEL STREET

Heaven's morning breaks

Berry Head, Brixham

The coastal waters of Torbay are sheltered by Berry Head, an elevated limestone promontory that juts into the English Channel like a protective arm. From its sculptured crags South Devon is laid out before you: moors to the north, rolling coast to east and west and, looking south, the restless open sea.

It's a place to watch the world go by: fishing boats hurrying towards the port of Brixham to land their catch, sailors rounding the headland on passage to the harbours of Dartmouth and Salcombe. Occasionally huge containerships draw close inshore to pick up Channel pilots to guide their voyage east. It is a crossroads of sorts, a place of change and transition, where a poet once penned immortal lines about his own final destination. His name was Henry Francis Lyte and the poem was "Abide with Me".

Berry Head sees a lot of weather. Seasons here are vivid and spectacular, their drama magnified by the headland's exposure and the diversity of wildlife, which, like flags, signal the unfurling year.

In spring great mackerel shoals arrive, churning the surface as they gorge on brit and sandeels. The frenzy excites the gannets and guillemots, which join the attack from above until the water boils. In the shallows, a strengthening sun ignites the food chain and soon the rock pools are brimming with life – bright red and green seaweeds providing cover for tom-pot blennies, starfish and anemones.

On land, the rich turf unpacks its secrets: sprays of white

"By July, Berry Head is beaming, its treasure chest of fauna and flora fully displayed."

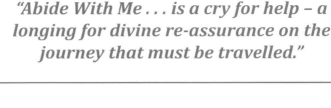

"Abide With Me . . . is a cry for help – a longing for divine re-assurance on the journey that must be travelled."

Henry Francis Lyte and (below) his vicarage, now the Berry Head Hotel

campions, sea pink and yellow vetch adorn the cliffs like flung cushions. Tender orchids show their heads and soon the calls of migrant birds – warblers, wheatears and terns – add the soundtrack of summer. By July, Berry Head is beaming, its treasure chest of fauna and flora fully displayed.

But nothing lasts. In August the swifts, sensing the shortening days, depart and soon they're joined by swallows and house martins, which roost among the headland's hawthorns and pylons before their long flight south. Nature shrinks, the energy that powered the lush green growth of spring retreats back into the earth. Then the storms of winter hurtle up the Channel, ending the cycle of the seasons with a roar of wind and spray. Stroll the headland in December and the delicate plants of summer have been trashed, their memory preserve in a few empty husks.

I've been coming to Berry Head for years, bird watching, fishing or just to admire the view. I proposed to my wife here, watched my daughter grow tall among its summer grasses, scattered the ashes of a friend. The passage of time seems amplified by the intensity of experience. Sunrise and sunset are massive and unavoidable, announcing across the whole panorama another day, another night, another solstice, another year. Like the storms of autumn there is no hiding from the sundial's sweeping hand. It is a place where the clock of our own mortality ticks loudly.

Henry Francis Lyte must have felt this too as he made his way each day from his town centre parish church of All Saints up the track to his vicarage tucked beneath the eastern parapet of Berry Head. He came to Brixham in 1826 to minister to the fishermen of the growing trawler fleet – a transient, impoverished community where life was hard and people died young. For every birth and baptism there was a burial and he must have shared many final hours.

In the 1840s Lyte himself fell sick, having

contracted tuberculosis, and the shadow of his own death began to reach out towards him. Like everyone else, he was afraid. Abide With Me, completed in those last months of his life, is a cry for help – a longing for divine re-assurance on the journey that must be travelled.

Swift to its close ebbs out life's little day
Earth's joys grow dim, its glories pass away:
Change and decay in all around I see,
O Thou who changest not, abide with me

But the verses also surge with an irrepressible hope, which this man of faith carried into the darkness.

I fear no foe with thee at hand to bless
Ills have no weight and tears no bitterness
Where is death's sting? Where grave thy victory?
I triumph still, if Thou abide with me.

Facing the mental and physical anguish of his own death, Lyte was able to articulate in simple, heart-felt words the hope expressed in all religions that life continues beyond it, that unlike the flowers of the headland we do not wither and die at the turn of the season.

Lyte placed into the hands of the English-speaking world a poem that has brought comfort at times of great trial. It was on the lips of First World War nurse Edith Cavell as she faced the firing squad, Shackleton's crew marooned on Elephant Island for many months drew strength from it and we chose the line "I triumph still" for my father's gravestone.

The last verse is the one most obviously inspired by the seascapes of Berry Head. During those last months Lyte must have spent many an anxious night longing for the light of dawn. And what a sight it would have been – the darkness of

"Unlike the flowers of the headland we do not wither and die at the turn of the season."

the eastern horizon slowly giving way to a pink glow until the tip of a great orange disk would slide out of the sea. Soon the foreboding silhouette of the headland would be bathed in gold. No wonder he could write with such passion:

"Heaven's morning breaks and Earth's vain shadows flee!
In life in death O Lord, abide with me!"

39

PICTURES: MATT ROUND

Warm glow of Christmas Eve

Exeter Cathedral

Summoned by bells from a Norman tower, I have hurried from the shopping malls of Exeter to the doors of its ancient cathedral. It's dusk on Christmas Eve and I'm waiting beneath its towering west front in a great throng of people queuing to get in.

In an age when church-going has declined, the prospect of standing room only in its vast interior is hard to fathom. But at Christmas, Devon's mother church draws crowds hungry for an experience which cannot be satisfied in the food halls and department stores of the modern city.

---

*"To sit in the nave of the 13th century
cathedral is to be at the heart
of a great forest of stone."*

I'm in at last, passing from the cold night air into the warm, candlelit interior. Before me lies a huge congregation sitting or standing wherever space allows. I have visited Exeter Cathedral many times, wondered at its stunning architecture and history, but like a fantastic piece of machinery, it is only truly impressive when it is doing what it was built for – as a place of worship.

I find a seat amongst the chattering, expectant congregation, greet an old friend and then try to clear my mind of the day's distractions to enjoy the occasion and its setting. To sit in the nave of the 13th century cathedral is to be at the heart of a great forest of stone. Columns carved with columns lead the eye ever upwards until the ribs fan out like boughs of trees to meet at a line of bosses. Looking down the nave I focus for a moment

"Through the arches of the choir screen, lights emerge, growing stronger in the gloom until the flickering glow illuminates the faces of a spellbound congregation."

on the intricate carving of the choir screen before the vaults ascend again in a vast avenue, replicating the same pattern into the distance. There's an organic quality to the cathedral, its lines and symmetry like the radials of a seashell that has grown enormous.

And everywhere is the clutter of the centuries, the tombs, plaques and memorial windows to the rich and famous, side chapels to a dozen saints, regimental colours, medieval clocks, carvings, corbels and crosses. The furniture of religion and its changing fashions is piled high, rich and enthralling like a family attic.

Christian history runs deep here. Roman graves unearthed in the Close lie east to west, the remains perhaps of the county's first converts. There was a monastery here in 670, an Anglo Saxon minster by 1050 and in the 12th century the Normans built the towers. But today's grandeur is the work of 13th century masons inspired to create in the medieval landscape an awe-inspiring centre of spiritual life. Seven hundred years later the landscape has changed beyond all recognition, but worshippers still flock to this holy acre seeking God.

The lights dim, the chamber falls silent and from the back of the cathedral the voice of distant choristers proclaim in Latin the Christmas message. "Today the Lord has

"The voices of a thousand people resound beneath the gothic vaults. Here is Devon at prayer"

shone upon us. Alleluia". And then, on this holiest of nights, the cathedral awakens. Through the arches of the choir screen, lights emerge, growing stronger in the gloom until the flickering glow illuminates the faces of a spellbound congregation. The voices of the choristers grow louder and soon they are among us, processing down the aisles in a parade of clergy in shining vestments holding high their banners of office. It's a spectacle straight out of the Middle Ages, rekindling in that dim light the awe in which the common man

43

must once have held the cloistered hierarchy of this mighty building.

But the days when Exeter Cathedral was the private church of bishop and priests, where the public could watch the services but rarely participate, are long gone and tonight the cathedral belongs to all who are gathered inside it.

And I sense the companionship of those around me, these fellow travellers who have also chosen to be here tonight singing carols, hearing the familiar verses of the Christmas story, seeking as I do a spiritual dimension to the celebrations. Within a church all are seekers, because the Christian God is never fully revealed, but glimpsed, like a distant light beyond the choir screen.

"The hopes and fears of all the years are met in thee tonight" run the words of the carol and we could as well be singing about ourselves as the voices of a thousand people resound beneath the gothic vaults. Here is Devon at prayer, our needs as diverse and complex as the contours of the county, but together in fellowship before God. It is a spiritual journey begun by Neolithic farmers as they gathered for their festivals among the standing stones of Merrivale and continued by the Celtic saints of North Devon into the chaos of the Dark Ages.

We do not journey alone, and as we stand to sing "Hark the Herald Angels Sing", the triumphant climax to the carol service, I add my small voice to the thunderous chorus: "Glory to the New-born King". And in this shared expression of joy I feel part of a people – a living, connected community – not just the harassed, isolated individual who had made his way here from the anonymous shopping arcades of Exeter.

Layer upon layer of history and tradition is stitched into the fabric of Exeter Cathedral. Like an old tree, its rings and scars record the changing seasons of religious belief and fashion, but 1500 years after the first foundations were laid, it remains a centre of Christian fellowship and worship. It is just a building, but people are drawn back year after year for a simple act: to stand together as one.

"The warmth of welcome at Lee Abbey radiates not from the fires in the hearth (though brightly they burn) but from the community that greets you"

Winter fire

Lee Abbey, nr Lynton

It's snowing. The sky is a cosmos of swirling flakes driven on by a brisk east wind, erasing the fussy detail of the land. Heath, hedge and highway are submerging beneath an icy blast leaving only a notion of themselves as bumps and creases.

I'm on my way to Lee Abbey near Lynton for a weekend retreat and been ambushed by bad weather on the fringes of Exmoor. I've followed a snow plough part of the way but the lumbering tractor has turned off and I'm left to negotiate the last few miles in the tracks of another vehicle. I reach the crossroads of Blackmoor Gate but on Wildner Top the road is exposed to drifting snow which plumes through gaps in the hedge building miniature mountain ranges across our path. The four-wheel-drive in front punches through them and I follow frantically behind while the snow grates beneath, like a toboggan.

Like most Devonians I love snow, waking up to find a dull, familiar view transformed by a heavy fall but on an open road with dusk falling, a Christmas card winter wonderland provokes high anxiety. I was hoping to arrive at Lee Abbey relaxed after a gentle drive – instead I skate into the car park like a terrified skier.

The warmth of welcome at Lee Abbey radiates not from the fires in the hearth (though brightly they burn) but from the community that greets you. It's a 100-strong comprising 17 different nationalities and of mainly young people who in exchange for food, lodging and dynamic fellowship, work six days a week hosting an endless procession of guests – like me. Only this weekend just five of us have made it through the weather.

Lee "Abbey" is misleading. It was built in Victorian times in the Gothic style as a private home, became a hotel, boys school during the war and finally, in 1945, bought by the Church of England as a conference centre. Half a million visitors later it is now an international movement, with outreach houses in the inner cities and a London hostel for foreign students. Members of the Devon community stay just one or two years and then, like sparks from a Catherine wheel, go off to fire up the faithful in a world which must seem as frozen and hostile as the Exmoor hills in winter.

In the morning I throw open the curtains a breathtaking view – meadows and woods giving way to dramatic coastal scenery – a setting so tranquil and extraordinary , a sense of separation from the mundane is instilled. Many of the places I've visited in this Devon odyssey have stirred wonder but the beauty around Lee Abbey feeds the spiritual life like a stream. Paths from the Abbey lead in all directions to little cliff top perches, viewpoints and sanctuaries where God's creation can be viewed and wondered at. What Devon inspires across many miles of stunning landscape can be explored here in miniature and in company. Many of my spiritual adventures have been solitary but here in Lee Abbey it is a shared encounter.

Here God is found together – during prayers, worship and spontaneous fellowship.

After breakfast I stroll outside. The hilltops remain in the grip of winter – frozen and lifeless even as the sun strengthens – but around the Abbey and along a narrow coastal strip the snow has melted creating a green oasis. Here the birds have gathered, flocks of lapwing and winter thrushes relishing the soft, thawed pastures where they can feed. The woods too are full of birds, tits and finches tumbling through the branches in huge numbers having flown the frozen waste.

I have all day – and no schedule as such – to wander the 268 acre estate, relax in the lounge, enjoy prayer times and communal meals. After lunch a Ugandan member of the community offers to show me the chapel on the beach created in the store house of abandoned lime kilns. In contrast to the Victorian grandeur of the Abbey here God is worshipped in simple walls, rough hewn and flagstoned beneath a barrelled roof, more a cave than chapel, where prayers are recorded with pebbles placed on a primitive altar. St Nectan would have been at ease among the stumps of candles, a battered Bible and with the roar of the sea in the distance.

An hour later and I've retreated in the comfort of Lee Abbey's library, sitting at a Queen Anne desk in a bay window with commanding views of the estate. The walls are lined with books reflecting 2000 years of earnest study where great

"Here God is worshipped in simple walls, rough hewn and flagstoned beneath a barrelled roof, more a cave than chapel"

minds have grappled with the mysteries of faith. If I were to read them all, would I be a wiser man? And with the snow still falling on the higher slopes and the forecast no better, I'm tempted to settle in an armchair by the fire, stretch out my legs and explore the trails blazed by others. In a world of struggle and strife where the ruthless prosper, and in which I often feel a fugitive, the serenity of this cloistered hall appeals like a glimpse of heaven. If God is encountered in quiet retreats then surely I'll meet him here.

But then the daily papers arrive like unwanted intruders with news as bleak as winter. Headlines in black heavy print shout of war and suffering, poverty and injustice, shattering the peace like a brick through the window. Sanctuary is an illusion, known only to those who can close their minds to the clamour beyond the walls. Lee Abbey provides just a brief one, preparing its visitors to return to the world and work with God to transform it.

I pick up the papers and sense their weight, like an overflowing inbox, and know I cannot stay. I spend my remaining hours seeking the spiritual fires of Lee Abbey in readiness to return to the cold.

"What Devon inspires across many miles of stunning landscape can be explored here in miniature and in company"

A shared meal at the old Torquay homeless hostel (not the group described here)

Sanctuary at the world's end

Factory Row homeless hostel, Torquay

I've left Devon's pretty places and postcard scenes, it's inspiring views and landmark churches.

Journey instead to central Torquay on a January night, to a back street overlooked by a multi-storey car park between the site of the town's old gasworks and a small hotel. Hear the noise from the pubs and the whirl of extractor fans in the backyards of takeaways; idling taxi engines; distant sirens. Someone is shouting, but their words are inaudible above the low din of urban life.

"The glow from the hostel windows has been like a beacon offering sanctuary when every other door is shut"

A stark orange lamp casts shadows along the ramshackle terrace until the road narrows beside the walls of a larger building. Its doors are covered by sheet steel and there are grills over the windows. We're going inside – into the old Factory Row homeless hostel – where I've had more encounters with the divine than on any winsome hill top.

The old hostel wasn't purpose-built, like the current one on the site, but converted from a disused mortuary in 1991 by a group of local churches determined to provide some shelter, however basic, for rough sleepers. I first went there as a journalist to report on its opening and it was then I met my first rough sleeper. The staff asked me if I would like to volunteer and so began a 20-year association.

We take a seat at the communal table for the evening

meal. Some men are already waiting, others emerge from the single dormitory. Eye contact is poor, the diners hesitant and watchful – people brought together by force of circumstance, disrupted lives which have converged like flotsam on a shore.

Conversation is difficult. Small talk seems trivial knowing the dramas and personal tragedies which have befallen some. Deeper questions seem intrusive, stirring raw feelings that the bearer may have fought all day anaesthetising with drugs or alcohol. Like fractured bones, they push beneath the skin, painful and ugly.

Faces mislead. The young lad with the funny T-shirt and the friendly smile watched his mum being beaten every week by his abusive father. He learned to smile to soften the blows when his father turned on him. Another man is chuckling, but the only voices telling jokes are the ones inside his head, so loud and disruptive he can't respond to mine.

And yet there is camaraderie at the world's end, glances of recognition of shared experiences on the joyless road to homelessness. Alone in tents, derelict hotels and doorways they were invisible and isolated – stripped of everything that bestows dignity – until they arrived here. I have welcomed men at the door on the worst of nights, when the glow from the hostel windows has been like a beacon offering sanctuary when every other door is shut.

It is a diverse family we've joined, from every walk of life. The gales that besiege the Hartland shore hammer relentlessly at all our lives and the strongest "citadels" can be overwhelmed in a hurricane of personal tragedies. The man sitting opposite was like you and I, until his child died and he turned to drink.

But recovery begins in places like this, first the companionship of those who have chartered similar depths but have breathed the air at the surface and will lead others to it. There are those who will hold another's pain and grieve with them – soul mates who know the value of tears.

I have seen in strangers' eyes an honesty that shines when all pretentions are stripped away and we connect at some deep level, spirit reaching out to spirit, open and unencumbered

The old Factory Row hostel, demolished to make way for the purpose-built Leonard Stocks centre which continues its work

–encounters as profound and moving as my time at Brentor or in the chapel at Buckfast. In such exchanges we discover our interdependence, our shared humanity – soul to soul while the storm of life rages on. The difference between us is in the breaking of a wave – one caught on the crest, the other sucked back on the undertow, yet if both reach out and hold tight neither should drown. Next time our positions could be reversed.

The meal is over, some people drift away, but a few stay and

"Recovery begins in places like this, first the companionship of those who have chartered similar depths but have breathed the air at the surface and will lead others to it"

---

talk in the communal lounge. Bill looks much older than his 43 years. His face bears the scars of falls or fights, his teeth stained by tobacco and drink. But alcohol has not dulled his wit or intelligence, and like the Ancient Mariner, he wants to tell his story.

"You don't sleep much outside; you're frightened of being kicked or having your things stolen. Then you get up and wander around but there's nothing to do. You're constantly outside and can't get warm. You feel things will never get better. Sleep deprivation destroys your mind. You get angry and paranoid. You lose what used to be you."

He fixes me with a stare. "I just want to be normal again", he says.

Then in a sharper tone he asks "Do you believe in God?" and you brace yourself for an avalanche of anger at a deity who appears to have done him no favours. But leaning forward he says intently: "I do, I pray every day"

And I know the God I've sought in scenic Devon countryside is encountered just as readily in the alleyways, shelters and parks of towns and cities by those who seek him. Maybe in hours of crisis, when vain ambitions and flimsy status are torn away, hearts are most receptive to divine help, when the call we may have heard all our lives but never answered, becomes irresistible.

As we leave he offers me his hand, a hand that has held on to God more tightly and in darker places than I have ever known, and in that rough, nicotine-stained hand I feel a firmness of grip passed on like a promise and a blessing.

NINA PANNELL

Waymarks of the high moor

Ter Hill, on the route of the Abbot's Way

I've returned again to the high moors, drawn to its wild space and raucous skies.

The claustrophobic, tomb-like days of winter have passed and a bright February morning offers hope of a long walk into the last great wilderness of southern England. I'm alone but not unguided, following a route laid down 800 years before by travelling monks.

The Abbot's Way is 24 miles long and links two of Devon's medieval abbeys – Tavistock and Buckfast. Following the Dissolution in 1541, both were abandoned (the current Buckfast Abbey was rebuilt in the 20th century), but we can follow in their footsteps today because across the landscape they raised a procession of rough-hewn stone crosses to mark the way. Centuries of robbing, vandalism and wild weather have taken their toll, but enough survive for an inspiring guided walk.

In a hollow just west of Coombeshead Tor, I pull on my walking boots and set out to complete the middle, and remotest stretch, of this ancient way. Within minutes I'm on to the wide expanse of Holne Moor, enjoying the freedom to roam in almost any direction with no barriers of human invention to restrain me. How used we are to the walls and channels of urban life, the gates and fences of lowland farming – how rare the open land.

And yet it also challenges us. Within minutes I've had to stop and pull out a map. And I'm not alone. A few hundred yards away a group of youngsters, practising for the annual Ten Tors walk, are fumbling with compasses. The high moors are disorientating, with few features to distinguish one hill from another, and when the mist comes down all sense of direction can be lost.

I pick up a path leading west, crossing a plain imprinted with 5,000 years of human history: a stone row older than the

> *"Horn's Cross. Like so many Dartmoor crosses its irregular lines and crude repair match the character of the setting – weather-worn and twisted like the hawthorns anchored on the hill"*

Pyramids; a reave built before the time of Christ; the remains of a cist belonging to a Neolithic hunter. Bronze age circles interlock with the beehive huts of tinners and medieval field systems, and through them weaves the Abbot's Way, a relative late-comer to the pattern of paths.

My attempt to follow it without modern navigational aids begins at Horn's Cross. Like so many Dartmoor crosses its irregular lines and crude repair match the character of the setting – weather-worn and twisted like the hawthorns anchored on the hill.

I'd hoped to see the next waymark clearly ahead but Down Ridge is bare of features and I set off uncertainly, descending at first to the O' Brook before climbing steeply again up a vast, anonymous hillside where the dead, colourless grass of winter stretches in all directions. Here the moor is like a desert: monotonous heath beneath a monotone sky, just the crunch of brittle grass breaking the silence.

There is no clear path, just dozens of minor ones worn by itinerant grazers that lead nowhere and my anxiety increases

when the weather worsens. Charging at me from the west is a storm cloud armed with hail, menacing the high moors like a predator. I'm caught in the open and can only turn my back to the assault and hope it passes. For five minutes the air fizzes with stinging ice – filling the creases of my clothes with tiny drifts until a burst of rain turns it to slush. By the time the storm has passed I'm cold, wet and more disorientated than ever.

I chance upon the Down Ridge cross by accident in a shallow featureless valley. It was in the wilderness, where there

ANDY PARROTT

56

are few natural landmarks, that they planted the crosses and its presence re-assures like a sign post on a lonely road. The Abbot's Way would once have been busy with wool jobbers, tin merchants and pack-horse drivers going about their business, but their journeys have long since ended.

I scan the horizon of low-slung hills. In the linear landscape the vertical line (however small) catches the eye and on the summit of one I glimpse a tiny fixture, a mile distant, beckoning me on. The sight of the distant cross, ancient and immovable, lifts my spirit and soon I'm springing up the hillside knowing each step is worthwhile and not misled like my dawdling on Down Ridge. I'm not the only one with wind in my sails. High above a pair of buzzards soar on the warming air.

Not that the going is easy. At one point I am forced to descend again, crossing marshland where a languid stream eases through rafts of sphagnum moss. There's a romantic notion that the monks followed the Abbot's Way engrossed in prayer and contemplation. More likely they were occupied

---

"The sight of the distant cross, ancient and immovable, lifts my spirit and soon I'm springing up the hillside"

with life's practicalities. Thoughts follow their own trails, the well-worn grooves of anxiety and reflection, and so we go on tramping down the years often oblivious to the paths we travel.

I'm walking strongly now to the summit of Ter Hill and the distant cross is growing in stature, taller than me, slightly crooked, a brush of yellow algae across its shoulders. It's held my gaze for the last hour over peat hags, mire and rocky ground, and I'm here at last. All around are expansive views of the southern moor, including the notorious Fox Tor Mire, and a bonus – a second cross, a hundred yards on, which would have guided travellers from the west.

Among blocks of black basalt I unpack my rucksack and am about to settle down to lunch when a stranger appears. "You're sitting on my geocache" he says. "Can I join you?" I welcome the company and over sandwiches and flasks of tea he explains how his GPS navigation aid has brought him to

these anonymous boulders to record his name in a moorland "letterbox" hidden beneath. The moor, he says, is covered with them. And he'd never be lost because an electronic screen displays his location.

We part with kind words, he clutching his bleeping compass, me looking for the waymark in the valley ahead – two men in a hostile land going our separate ways. I envied him his new technology, his certainty of step, but reflected that one day the satellites might fall from the sky and maps and guide books perish in the libraries. But the granite sentinels would still stand tall.

Worshippers of a shingle island

Saltstone, nr Kingsbridge

At the junction of three muddy creeks in a Devon estuary is a weed-strewn tidal island which at high water disappears. It is called the Saltstone and a more cheerless place is hard to imagine. But in the 17th century at the height of religious strife in England this lonely spot was holy ground, a refuge to a band of non-conformists who could gather safely nowhere else.

Cromwell was dead, the Civil War was passing into memory and Charles II had restored the monarchy. The evangelical, free-thinking Puritans were in retreat and conservative forces unleashed a series of repressive laws to crush their influence. Clergy faced a simple choice – conform to a traditional pattern of worship, swear allegiance to the king or be thrown out of your church. More than 2,000 refused and lost their livelihoods.

But it got worse. Act followed Parliamentary Act driving these non-conformists further into the wilderness and banning

them from going within five miles of their former parishes and most towns. If they convened religious meetings of more than five people, they and their followers faced fines or imprisonment.

Devon ports like Plymouth and Dartmouth which had long harboured a dissenting spirit now found many of their religious leaders banished or cowed. From then on they had to find remote locations, beyond the reach of the King's men, to worship freely. And so a tidal bank, outside the boundary of any parish or Magistrate's jurisdiction, became the most precious acre on God's earth to South Devon's Christian outcasts.

"I see their ghosts, drawing towards the Saltstone in their small boats like refugees, the clunk and splash of oar growing louder as they approach."

It's early March and I've arrived by boat, having set off from Kingsbridge an hour earlier. You can also reach the Saltstone on foot either from Frogmore or West Charleton when the tide permits. It's a messy place to land, a fringe of squidgy mud at low water has to be negotiated before you reach the firmer rock. But this too is hazardous, covered in a tangle of bladderwrack and bootlace weed that slips and slides. Occasional holes ensnare you. Only after a precarious scramble do you reach a tiny crest of shingle, no more than a few feet across, and firmer footing.

The tide has dropped, revealing a broad arena of creeks, pools and mudbanks which have grown ever more expansive with the falling tide. Everywhere there are wading birds browsing the flats for any worms, fish or other morsels they can find. It is a rich habitat and the air is full of their calls.

Looking down stream I can see the lower stretches of the Kingsbridge estuary crowded with expensive yachts moored alongside houseboats the size of London flats. Beyond them, Salcombe and the most valuable real estate in England creeping up the hill. But the surge and excess of modern living has yet to spoil the upper reaches of the estuary and the neat fields, ancient woodland, copse and creek of an older England fold around me.

It looks idyllic today in early spring sunshine, but to the persecuted non-conformist it was a hostile land where oppressors roamed armed with a tyrant's power to imprison and possess. They did not come as I have, on an idle jaunt, but impassioned and fearful, risking freedom for their faith, a group cast out from the world that once embraced them. While others compromised they could not.

And in my mind's eye I see their ghosts, drawing towards

the Saltstone in their small boats like refugees, the clunk and splash of oar growing louder as they approach the one place they could gather freely. They would have come from all over Devon, the time and place spoken of in whispers, many taking days to get here. I see them land and embrace, kindred spirits banished to a windswept island far from home.

How they must have sung, prayed, preached and implored their God even as the changing season hurled foul weather over the mudflats, shredding their earnest words. Looking north they would have glimpsed the tower of Kingsbridge church and remembered the warm interiors of their own churches, now barred to them.

"How the congregation must have drawn closer as the tide encroached, a shrinking band of figures precarious and lonely in the expanding flood, holding on to their precious acre."

I've stayed too long, and the rising tide has begun to lift my small boat off the shore until it tugs urgently at the painter. Wading birds are moving too, flying up the creeks to reach the last exposed mudflats and their high-water roosts. Channels around the Saltstone begin to swirl with murky water, until it overwhelms the narrow isthmus.

How the congregation must have drawn closer as the tide encroached, a shrinking band of figures precarious and lonely in the expanding flood, holding on to their precious acre. And their voices, carrying over the water, praising God.

Many tides have ebbed and flowed since then. Persecution gave way to tolerance, and the non-conformists would eventually build their own chapels and meeting houses alongside the parish churches. Memories of oppression would grow dim as comfort and security increased.

But their place on the Saltstone would be taken by others – persecuted minorities the world over who have been driven to the edge. And while the non-conformists and I took to our boats just as the last footholds were lost, there would be no escape for some in the wrenching currents of history.

Power within a sleepy chapel

Loughwood, nr Axminster

Loughwood Meeting House, three miles east of Axminster, stands in rolling hills – its stone and whitewashed walls snuggling beneath a roof of thatch surrounded by flower meadows. A more idyllic spot would be hard to find.

But the serenity is deceptive, for this tiny Baptist chapel, preserved by the National Trust, is a remnant of a revolution where big ideas and religious manifestos were born and a spirited community struggled with conflict and persecution. Even today, visitors should approach with caution for there is power here trying to get out!

Loughwood was built in the latter half of the 17th century when non-conformist congregations could no longer worship freely. As we have seen, in South Devon dissenters took to the tidal Saltstone to escape the jurisdiction of the county sheriff. In East Devon it was the deep woods around Axminster that provided protection.

The trees have long gone, but the building still keeps a low profile, tucked into the hillside down a narrow lane, with two small parking spaces for visitors. But few come to explore, and with heavy rain forecast I sense I will be the only one this day.

The interior is intimate, like stepping into a house, with the bare functionality of a town hall or school room. Natural

"A tall, prominent pulpit towers above the room like the prow of a ship"

light streams in from six large windows, creating a cheerful ambience. Everything is neat and ordered, a first-floor gallery looking down on rows of box pews focused on a tall, prominent pulpit that towers above the room like the prow of a ship. The meeting house hasn't been used for regular services since 1969, when the local Baptist church handed the keys to the National Trust, but there remains an expectation that something is about to happen.

I settle into a box pew, closing the door quietly so as not to disturb the silence. The panelling inside is simple, unvarnished and with no concession to comfort. This was a place to hear the word of God and act upon it, not to relax in a cushioned seat. During the early years, membership was strong with over 200 attending, many travelling great distances to get here. It would have been a crowded, excited place coursing with religious fervour and solidarity. But in later years the chapel settled into a predictable cycle of decline and resurgence depending on leadership and circumstances. Now all is still save for the hands of the clock at the front of the gallery, counting through the empty hours.

Bare walls stare at bare walls beneath a simple whitewashed ceiling. With no ornamentation to interest the eye I stare at the wood patterns on the bench in front of me. How familiar the knots and grain would have been to the families who sat here, week after week, year after year from childhood to old age. Their hopes and fears would have been unburdened here in spoken prayers and private thoughts. Favourite hymns would have been sung with joy and defiance.

But these boards would also have soaked up the longings of the heart and caught the tears of the bereaved. The wooden rails would have supported the crippled hands of the aged worshipper kneeling at their last communion. There are no memorials to them. The only plaque inside is to a favourite pastor who died in 1778. Loughwood Meeting House was built to save the living, not commemorate the dead.

I look out of the window. The rain is falling steadily now, denying views of distant hills, so I'm drawn back to the dominant feature of the chapel – the central, elevated pulpit from where the pastor would have delivered his thunderous sermons. Perched on its apex, overhanging the inadequate lectern, is a huge King James' Bible. It's open, invitingly, on what page I wonder? No other book has so occupied the human mind or influenced the course of history, and it sits provocatively a few feet away, demanding attention.

I climb the three short steps to take a closer look, old timbers creaking beneath my feet. The bible's heavy bound

"*Perched on its apex, overhanging the inadequate lectern, is a huge King James' Bible*"

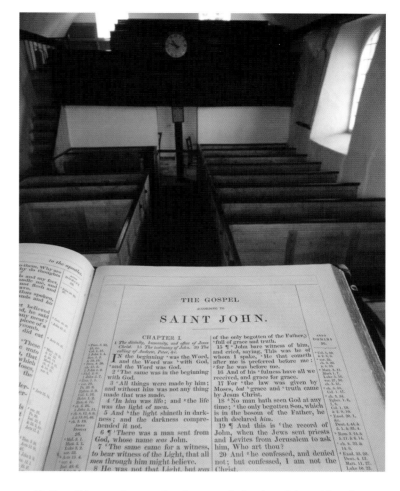

pages are well-fingered and much read, left open at the Gospel of St John and its profound opening line "In the beginning was the word . . .".

Then in my mind's eye the people are crowding into the church again – eager for this word to be read, a 21st century congregation that has mapped the human genome, solved the mysteries of the natural world and probed the fringes of outer space but cannot discern a purpose. But who will read? I'm suddenly conscious, standing here in the pulpit of a church, of my own cowardice and shortcomings to expound the word of God to a disbelieving world.

And yet it is a book that has shaped human morality, brought joy and salvation to millions and inspired the oppressed in the darkest of times. It's incited revolutions and loosed the grip of earthly power. Today its pages spark with radical ideas that are deeply subversive of modern "wisdom" challenging our priorities and pre-occupations, raging against wealth and inequality, demanding action now – with a siren urgency that the leather binding can barely hold.

This is no dusty tome but a ticking time bomb, the charge beneath the city walls of our materialistic age waiting to go off. The 17th century evangelists are long gone, but their ammunition is live and ticking. Loughwood Meeting House should have a cordon around it and visitors warned "*Approach with caution – unexploded ordnance on the pulpit. Enter at your own ris*k"

Before I leave, I record a few words in the visitors' book, which sits neatly beside a vase of fresh flowers. Those who have written before describe the chapel as tranquil, peaceful, "a place for quiet reflection". I issue a bomb warning. Loughwood is ready to blow.

MIKE SMITH

The edge of knowledge
Eddystone lighthouse

Embark now in a small boat to reach the last piece of Devon, a fragment to the distant south swept by waves and currents, where man's presence is infrequent and precarious.

The Eddystone is at the very edge, 13 miles south west of Plymouth, and visible only from land on a clear day by the 160ft lighthouse which stands upon it. For the day tripper there is no further destination, beyond lies the open ocean and unreachable shores. We journey because it is the edge. Man's desire to explore seems only satisfied at the mountain's summit, or river's source when the final corner is turned and there are no more paths to tread or courses to steer.

It is at these points that journeys feel complete. We attain some vantage point that gives perspective to our striving and geography to our lives.

So my friend Nigel and I put to sea in a 16ft sailing boat from the creek at Newton Ferrers on a warm June day encouraged by settled weather and a westerly breeze strong enough to carry us there, but not overpower us. The passage is not without hazard. Many would consider the Drascombe Dabber under-sized for an off-shore trip, but I'm with a friend who has spent many years sailing these waters and knows well the reefs and pinnacles of Wembury Bay which lie like snares just below the surface.

This is also my shore. Strong childhood friendships were

"An ebb tide carries us downstream through the moored boats of the Pool."

forged in fishing and camping expeditions along this coast, when we put to sea in dinghies daring to venture beyond the bar where the ocean swells rolled and beckoned. We played in the shallows where sun danced over golden sands but our imaginations swam in the dark water where the monsters lurked.

I must have been nine or ten, climbing the headland at Gara Point, when I first noticed the Eddystone Light. At first it appeared like the mast of a ship, only it didn't move, and having stood at the base of Smeaton's Tower on Plymouth Hoe and seen how big lighthouses were, I sensed its remoteness and wanted to get there.

Lying in bed on wind-lashed nights I imagined the lighthouse keepers at their watch, praying their remote citadel would survive as every roller sent a shudder through the tower. It hadn't always. The current lighthouse is the fourth. The first, timber-framed Winstantley Tower, was completed in 1698 but five years later a violent storm charged up the Western Approaches and the elegant construction was swept away with the loss of all lives. Rudyard's lighthouse stood from 1709-

1755 until destroyed by a fatal fire. The famous Smeaton's Tower survived the worst Atlantic storms for 120 years until cracks appeared in the foundation rock. It was dismantled to be reassembled on Plymouth Hoe and a new lighthouse built nearby. It has stood for 135 years and is now fully automated.

Today the sea is in a gentle mood. An ebb tide carries us downstream through the moored boats of the Pool, over the shallow spit of Warren Point towards the mouth of the estuary. The first glimpse of open water stirs excitement and trepidation. The Mewstone, lush with summer vegetation, rises steep and majestic, but reefs – like shark fins – break surface in a menacing row east to west.

We anchor in Cellars Cove, to stow gear, plot a course and raise the sails. Unfurling a mainsail is to harness a fickle power which has propelled great adventures, carried fleets around the world, but becalmed as many miles from land. Mariners pore over pressure charts, study the clouds, but the wind has no master. And when the gale comes there is no shelter from the storm, no throttle to ease or handbrake to pull, just the frantic reefing of sails and battening down of hatches until the

"The first glimpse of open water stirs excitement and trepidation."

*"I trail my fingers like the old
mariners would trail a ship's log and
feel the water rush through them, sensing
the journey cable by cable."*

danger has passed. I remember a day, as tranquil as this, when
we lazed on decks beneath full sails trolling lines for mackerel,
when a squall charged from the south and almost capsized us.

This morning the horizon is clear and the first punch of air
sends us surging, in engine-less silence, out to sea. Beneath
us, fathom by dark fathom, the land slides away. Soon the
cliffs are an indistinct line on the horizon and we pass onto a
strange, unfamiliar plain without waymarks where the blue of
the sea reflects on the blue of the sky and we skip the surface
without consequence, an ephemeral footprint pressed on water
and air. I trail my fingers like the old mariners would trail a
ship's log and feel the water rush through them, sensing the
journey cable by cable. The tower of the Eddystone Light, so
distant to start with, is growing larger and the tide is with us.

Soon the water is deeper than the anchor can plumb.
Sunlight penetrates a few metres to illuminate the alien shapes
of barrel jellyfish, the size of dustbins, pulsing beneath us . We
can see no further. In the deep abyss, hidden from our gaze,
are stranger creatures and unfathomable forms. Only on calm
days when the sea is like a mirror do curious patterns swirl
across the surface hinting at cliffs and caverns far beneath – an
unseen world scribbling messages to navigators above.

We journey on. I am further out than I have ever been in so
small a boat. Old perspectives change. Devon, the chocolate
box county I have travelled these many years, is almost lost
in the haze yet I find myself looking back for the familiar and
assured. Is that Brentor in the distance? The spire of Charles
Church catching the morning sun? Yet I'm drawn to the
distant rock with its great white tower, where the endless battle
between man and nature plays out at its most ferocious, where
the pioneers raised their stones to stand taller than any wave –
and lit a lamp.

But that will be for another day. Inexplicably the wind
drops, the sails begin to flap and with the tide turning against
us we must head for home just a few miles short of our
destination. Someone looking down from a great height would
have seen a speck of a boat on a vast ocean turn 180 degrees
and track slowly back.

We shall not cease from exploration... and one day a
wind will fill our sails and carry us further than we've ever
imagined. For now, two old friends sit in a creek-side pub with
a pint of cider enjoying a little of heaven on earth.

JON-PAUL HEDGE

Lights in the heavens

Beardown Man, Dartmoor

In 1885, the Dartmoor writer William Crossing, came across a remote standing stone in the wilderness of the northern moor. As the sun cast its dying beams he wrote:

"As it was to the patriarchs of old, so it is to us now. It is a pillar of witness – a witness that those who reared it looked above the earth on which they trod. Looked upward and found a hope, as we may do to-day, for it is a finger that points from that which perishes, and where the day becomes spent, and loses itself in darkness, to a kingdom of light that shall endure forever".

He was writing about the Beardown Man, an eleven-foot-high block of granite raised by human hands 4,000 years ago for reasons long forgotten. Unlike the stone rows of Merrivale or the menhirs of Drizzlecombe, it is not connected with any Bronze Age settlements but stands alone, the highest monument on Dartmoor, commanding views in all directions. Was it a waymark or meeting place, used for religious ceremony or just good parties?

I first came upon it many years ago while hiking between Fur Tor and Two Bridges. We'd trudged for miles over featureless peat bog, with mist coming and going, and then the great stone reared up ahead and we knew exactly where we were. Today I've come from the opposite direction with a friend, to enjoy the landscape at sunset and a night sky beyond the glare of city lights.

We arrive for day's grand finale, the clouds ablaze with colour until the sun emerges from behind the scenes, full and golden, for the curtain call. The star of the show takes a final bow from the silhouetted steps of Great Mis Tor and slips away. Immediately it feels colder, the grass of the open moor that was charged with gold minutes earlier now looks white and haggard like old man's beard and the rocks of Devil's Tor behind us lose their texture to become a shadowy presence.

"We arrive for day's grand finale, the clouds ablaze with colour until the sun emerges from behind the scenes, full and golden, for the curtain call"

We had hoped for a clear night to watch the stars switch on one by one, but clouds build from the west and darkness falls suddenly, dispiritingly. The distant views are gone, and soon our world has shrunk to the length of a torch beam.

We seek shelter from the wind among the granite stacks of Devil's Tor, finding one just big enough to shield our stove and brew some tea. This gesture of civilisation in the Dartmoor wilderness, briefly lifts our spirits. We share food and tell stories, as Mesolithic hunters would have done around their fires four thousand years before. As the night deepens, starless and cold, I'm grateful for the company. Then Jon-Paul falls asleep and I'm left contemplating the darkness alone.

To the west is the thinnest band of light, between the cloud cover and the horizon, as the last energy of the day drains from the world and against it I catch the profile of the Beardown Man, upright and immovable. Apart from the lights of Hessary Tor, it is the only reference point, the sole focus in a deepening void. As colourful sunsets stir the imagination and inspire lofty thoughts, so darkness depresses them. I feel like a prisoner in a windowless cell. Night has become a dungeon. Then the walls explode. Suddenly a fireball crosses the sky illuminating not just the clouds but the whole landscape. "Did you see that?" exclaims Jon-Paul who is suddenly wide awake and pointing skyward. "The biggest shooting star I've ever seen." Remarkably, our midnight rendezvous with the Beardown Man has coincided with a major astronomical event, observed across the south of England: a fragment of Haley's Comet crashing to Earth. The heavens have awakened and within minutes the veil of cloud draws back allowing the first stars of a yet far greater wonder to appear.

The night sky is the most profound of revelations, yet rarely do we stand in awe of it, opening our minds and imaginations to the distance and complexity. To our primitive ancestors it must have been a familiar spectacle, but they knew nothing of the vastness of space, of the millions of galaxies which spiral away into the distant cosmos that we now marvel at through powerful telescopes.

Yet from the beginning man has looked upwards to understand our place in the universe, where knowledge and mysteries intertwine like constellations. The wisest of stargazers have seen enough to realise we know little, that the further we peer into space and time the greater the puzzle. And what of the bigger questions beyond the scope of science and philosophy that seek to explain the purpose of this stellar creation? Why there is something rather than nothing? As we sit and ponder, I focus again on the silhouette of the Beardown Man etched now against a cloud of stars, like a bookmark in a vital page, pointing heavenward.

ALEX NAIL

Despite our euphoria at having witnessed a cosmic event, both of us are getting cold and we turn for home, following a compass bearing across the dark expanse of moor. The clouds continue to come and go, driven like ghosts across the stars and with fading torches we blunder into the usual hazards, difficult to negotiate in day, and worse at night.

At last the ground becomes more even, rising gently to an elevated amphitheatre ringed by the dim peaks of Beardown Tor. During the hour since we left, the stars have become more brilliant and once again a break in the cloud throws open the glory of the heavens framed by granite towers. We stand bedazzled, feasting our eyes on the great constellations, star clusters and distant nebulae and arched across them all is the glow of the Milky Way.

In this throne room of the cosmos I sense the presence of the architect who wills us to lift our heads from the mundane and worldly, and to meditate on the infinite and unfathomable. And I glimpse my place in this universe, a child of God destined to stand at the summit of creation, sentient and searching. Through us the universe has become conscious of itself and staring up into the great beyond, I believe its creator is conscious of me.

"The night sky is the most profound of revelations, yet rarely do we stand in awe of it"

73

Snapsh of Staines

J.L. & D.M. Barker

INTRODUCTION

Such is the current pace of change that the approaching new millennium seems an appropriate time to remember that previous eras saw their own transformations. What better way to recall these more recent changes than to reflect, via the medium of the photograph, the dramatic alterations that have occurred in Staines during the last century and a half. Both Parish and town have exercised great fascination for historians over the years which, coupled with the exciting archaeological discoveries during the last 40 years, have shown that the area has a remarkable heritage to carry into the next phase of its existence. In fact, Staines has been the subject of many fine publications in recent years, and to Barry Dix and Graham Smeed in particular we express our sincere thanks for their unstinting help and enthusiasm and for enabling us to continue their work of bringing the town's photographic heritage to a wider audience. To Spelthorne Museum, and the volunteers to whose generous sacrifice of their time and effort it owes its continued existence, we would also like to express our heartfelt gratitude.

One continuing aspect of the town has been its consistent importance as a transport hub and as a commercial centre. We have also been delighted to illustrate some of its remarkable industrial heritage and hope that this snapshot of an ancient and continually evolving community will provide further evidence of the value of the photograph as an historical tool.

As with our previous publications, we have tried to gather images from all periods and aspects of the area and hope that this compilation will provide pleasure and interest to both older and newer residents of Staines. Any one wishing to learn more of the town's fascinating history is urged to visit the Spelthorne Museum, housed in the Old Fire Station, adjacent to the Old Town Hall, where displays and temporary exhibitions cover many aspects of the Borough's and town's heritage.

Jocelyn and David Barker
November 1999

FRONT COVER
1. Town Hall and Market Square c.1905
2. Congregational Church, Thames Street, c.1907
3. Linoleum Factory from the Brewery Tower c.1930
4. River Thames, October 1999
5. In the reserve is the badge used by the Staines Parish Council and Urban District Council until 1951.

TOWN HALL c.1885

The Surrey bank of the Thames gives an excellent vantage point from which to admire the late Victorian vista of Staines Town Hall and its environs. Indeed, the juxtaposition of the civic and commercial aspects of the town is well illustrated here. Both the Town Hall and the headquarters of the town's volunteer fire brigade are recent structures on the riverside, together with the newly-planted belt of trees. Just visible at the rear of the brigade headquarters are two items of their equipment – a ladder and what appears to be the 1738 manual engine, now restored and on display in the Old Fire Station, which houses Spelthorne Museum. The adjacent yard of William Ridley & Sons, timber merchants, also indicates the importance of the Thames as a commercial highway allowing substantial loads to be delivered to the heart of the town.

TOWN HALL AND SWAN UPPERS c.1975

Seen travelling upstream is the skiff leading the annual visitation of the Swan Uppers. The flotilla of boats was led by that bearing the Sovereign's emblem, followed by those of the Vintners' and Dyers' Companies of the City of London. This ceremony involves surveying and marking the cygnets of previously marked birds and is normally carried out in the third week of July. Their route from London to Henley passes a wide range of riverside scenery, and that of the Staines stretch of the Thames encompasses both meadows and urban vistas. Staines Town Hall, although more usually pictured from its frontage to the Market Square, also has an attractive rear elevation. Many of the huts and outbuildings seen here have been cleared, although the gabled single storey of the Old Fire Station is still extant.

RIVER THAMES, March 1947

Previous historic and prehistoric inundations have left tangible evidence of the power of the Thames and its tributaries to bring severe disruption to human settlements in their vicinity. Although the causeway constructed from the old Staines Bridge to the foot of Egham Hill in the 13th century is still tangible, many of the other flood control features around Staines itself are less well known. The outfall of the Colne at Staines also adds to the intensity of the local effects of any flooding on the inhabitants of Staines. A spectacular demonstration of the severity of the 1947 flood is this low-level view of the Middlesex and Surrey banks of the Thames. This modern flood began in March and followed the sudden thaw of the extremely bad winter just endured. A permanent reminder of the seriousness of the inundation is to be seen in the Church Street registering board in the River Colne, which records that

the water levels were even worse than those experienced during the 1894 disaster, although it appears that some inaccuracy arose from the board's having been removed and replaced at the wrong height. Other local watercourses also contributed to the situation and contemporary reports speak of Leacroft being reminiscent of Venice, with water 5 ft. deep in places and 4 ft. of water under the Thames Street railway bridge. Eventually, over 1,000 of the 8,250 acres in the S.U.D.C. area were submerged for a week. The water finally began to subside at the end of March, by which time over 75 families had been evacuated to emergency accommodation including the Town Hall and Duncroft. Cost to the ratepayers was estimated to be at least £10,000; and in still-rationed Britain, while the Council issued free disinfectant, soap was made available at 6d (2½ p) per lb. (454 gm) without coupons.

BIFFEN'S BOATYARD c.1956

Although the Thames had always served as a convenient and strategic highway, only in the latter part of the 19th century did it become the focus of a leisure industry. This, based around pleasure boating, led to a huge number of specialist boat builders and hirers. Biffen's Yard had originally been founded c.1880 by Adolphus Snelson in a prime position just up-stream from Staines Bridge and was later run by W.C. Pinchen. Although it was apparently on the Surrey bank, the original course of the river ran behind the site and what became an eyot was originally a mid-stream island and part of the Parish of Staines. Also seen in the photograph is part of the western abutment of the wooden and steel wartime emergency crossing colloquially known as the "Bailey Bridge", although its proper design designation was a "Callender-Hamilton" type.

STAINES BRIDGE, January 1963

Although it has been many years since the area has experienced such severe weather conditions as to freeze the Thames, the winter of 1962-63 remains an indelible memory for many. Snow started to fall on Boxing Day 1962, heralding the coldest winter locally since 1940. This photograph by Alan Hobbs shows workers from the adjacent Petters works on the ice-bound river. Such scenes were repeated at many sites along the Thames, although there appear to be no reports of consequent accidents.

CLARENCE STREET 1880s

The foundation stone of the handsome building on the corner of Clarence Street was laid in 1835 by the Right Hon. Sir W.H. Fremantle. It was built as the headquarters of the Literary and Scientific Institute, founded in the latter part of 1834, and in the late 19th century it housed the Liberal Club. Later it became a piano showroom and, by 1908, a printing and newspaper office. In the 1930s it became an antique shop called the Griffyn Gallery and from 1939 was utilised as a strong-point for the defence of Staines Bridge. In May 1948, the "Middlesex Chronicle" reported a plan to convert the building into the town's first Public Library. The library remained here until it moved into the Oast House in Kingston Road in 1979. Nearby are the original premises of the Staines and Egham Industrial Co-operative Society Limited, which had opened here in 1880. Opposite is Bridge House, built soon after 1832 by Randolph Horne, Clerk to the Bridge Commissioners, on surplus land bought from the Commissioners. .

CLARENCE STREET c.1910

Clarence Street was created as an approach road to the present Staines Bridge. This wintry scene shows the Bridge House Hotel in the right foreground. Bridge House was purchased by Tom Taylor and converted into a hotel about 1897 and became the scene of numerous garden parties, dances, concerts and other social events. Between the hotel and the bridge he set up a boatyard where he built houseboats and steamers. Later, a garage was opened in connection with the hotel. By 1914, this was being used as the starting point for tours by the Motor Cycling Club, bringing good business for James Brown, licensee of the hotel from 1911 when Tom Taylor sold it. In the later 1920s the business fell into financial difficulties and in 1929 was put into the hands of an Official Receiver. It closed in 1937 and was demolished in 1938. Beyond the Hotel is Colne Lodge.

CLARENCE STREET c.1967

By the time this view was recorded, the Library was well established in the former Literary and Scientific Institute, while opposite, the Bridge House Hotel had been replaced by the present large cinema (see below). The original site of the London Stone was approximately where the back of this building now stands. Colne Lodge, beyond, had also been demolished. Near the library, in the former Co-operative Society premises, can be seen Dobson's Garage, which in April 1931 was the first Staines business to install neon lighting – a large orange and blue sign much admired by the local Press! This car showroom remained in operation until 1988, after which the firm concentrated its business at the Egham branch. Another first in Clarence Street was the town's original Telephone Exchange, situated near the Colne bridge.

REGAL CINEMA 1939

A typical late-1930s cinema, the Regal was designed by William R. Glen, House Architect for the ABC (Associated British Cinema) chain and opened on 20th February, 1939, with Cary Grant and Katharine Hepburn in "Free to Love" and Peter Lorre in "Mysterious Mr. Moto". The 1,613 seats were priced at 6d., 1s., 1s. 6d. and 2s. (2½ p-10p), and a free car park was provided for patrons. On 30th May, 1970, it closed for "twinning", the former circle becoming the 586 seat "ABC 1" and the stalls the "ABC 2", with 694 seats. The latter was further divided in November 1972, re-opening on 22nd January, 1973, as ABC 2 and ABC 3, with 361 and 174 seats respectively. The cinema was renamed the Cannon in 1986, MGM in 1993, and is now the ABC again. It is currently (October 1999) threatened with demolition.

CLARENCE STREET c.1905

Circuses were regular visitors to the area, the animals (with the exception of slow or dangerous creatures such as sea lions and big cats) being led or ridden from town to town. The result was a spectacular parade which served as free publicity for the forthcoming entertainment. This parade is entering Staines along Clarence Street, the camels in the distance just crossing the bridge over the Colne. The nature of the acts is illustrated by publicity for a visit of Sanger's Circus in 1915, when they put on two performances on Good Friday at Greenlands Road Meadow, Kingston Road. Attractions included a Russian Cossack display, the Elephants' Gymnasium, a wire-walking elephant, Sanger's Marvellous Performing Sea-lions, Goliath the giant horse with Peter Pan the midget pony, the Six Fonsons bare-back riders, (two of them ladies), the Aerial Danes and the Two Willies (clowns) with Caesar the lion and Pasha the camel.

BRIDGE STREET c.1932

The London General Omnibus Company service no. 61 is waiting to start on its hourly service to Kingston. The "S"-type single-decker was one of 48 operated by the Company and first introduced in 1923. Some of these were housed at the Weybridge Garage ("A Window on Weybridge", p.6), as indicated by the stencilled WB plate on the waist-rail. Staines' first motor bus services pre-dated the First World War. Gardam & Sons ran a service between Staines and Egham with room for eight passengers, but were notorious for being somewhat inefficient and liable to fail to arrive at all. By the time of the opening of the new facility in London Road (page 42), the town had the services of seven independent companies ranging from one-man, one-vehicle enterprises to large regional operators. This network was rationalised by the purchase of many firms by the new London Passenger Transport Board in 1932. Bridge Street, however, continued as a departure point regulated by the provision of an official omnibus stop here in 1933.

HALE STREET c.1910

There is still a bridge over the Wyrardisbury River and some of the buildings in the right foreground survive, but nothing else remains to recall the days when these workers from the Linoleum Factory made their way home from work along Hale Street. The row of cottages on the left, known as Lino Cottages, together with some cottages in Factory Path, housed some of the workers, including the factory firemen, who might be urgently needed on site at any time! In 1930, some 26 households were listed in Hale Street – a contrast with the somewhat bleak vista of today. The elegant gas lamp standard has the names of the streets across the top of the glass on each side. Passing behind it are two boys with a handcart, possibly collecting horse manure from the roads to sell for pocket money. One local man in 1993 recalled collecting manure from the Moor to sell to Sir Frank Swettenham of Duncroft at about 6d. (2½ p) per barrow-load.

HALE STREET c.1910

Although current agricultural shows and the annual Easter Parade in Battersea Park still feature classes for horse-drawn turn-outs, at one time such displays were commonplace. The vehicle, driver and horses were all an advertisement for their respective businesses and keen competition ensued. Indeed, this smart van may have been the product of one of the local coach builders. The local event at which J.F. Harris' bread van probably won its First Prize was the Staines, Egham and District Horse Parade, at which Class D was for "tradesmen's cobs or ponies single undecorated in van or trade cart". This event seems to have commenced in 1900. Held on Whit Monday morning, it was a regular spectacle for the inhabitants of Staines and District, who could also attend the comprehensive programme of events organised in connection with the Linoleum Sports Day held in the afternoon. John Francis Harris' premises at 17, High Street, were rebuilt in the mid-1950s and occupied by Dexter's.

ASHBY'S MALT HOUSE AND BREWERY TOWER c.1990

Ashby's Staines Brewery was founded by Thomas Ashby of 57, Church Street. By 1796 he was described as a maltster and may have built this malthouse in Moor Lane, used until 1921. He started brewing in his kitchen and subsequently moved the venture to the other side of the road, going into partnership with two of his sons to create the company which lasted until 1931. In 1898 they were advertising beer in the new screw-stoppered bottles ranging in price from 2s. 3d. (12p) to 4s. 6d. (22½ p) per dozen. The Brewery Tower in Church Street, now converted to apartments, dates to 1903. In that year they bought Harris's brewery at Knowle Green (closed c.1912), and with it, 39 further inns and beerhouses to add to the many they already owned. The Church Street brewery was taken over by H. & G. Simmonds of Reading in 1931, and they in turn by Courage. Brewing ceased here in the 1950s and in the 1970s the buildings were converted into offices. All except these were demolished in 1987.

ENGINE ROOM, ASHBY'S BREWERY 1928

The greater part of Ashby's Brewery had been rebuilt in 1903 "on modern lines", and in 1928 the company considered itself "one of the most up-to-date establishments of its kind in the country". A further building had just been completed, giving facilities for trebling the output of bottled beers. The water for their "Charta" ales was drawn from an artesian well 360 ft. deep, delving beneath the London Clay and was considered absolutely pure. Bottling was by this time completely mechanised, including the washing – an important process at a time when beer bottles were returnable. The necessary machinery for this and other processes was powered by the large engines shown here.

CHURCH STREET c.1905

A favourite scene for postcard producers, this part of Church Street has kept much of its former character, but is not altogether unchanged. Of the houses in the left foreground, the only ones surviving are numbers 72 and 74. Further away, Cambria House, then the home of the brewer Charles Ashby, has been replaced by the present Cambria Court. The pinnacles on the church tower were removed following bomb damage in the Second World War. Two more houses seen here were once occupied by the Ashby family: the wisteria-covered Corner Hall and The Beeches (no. 113), then occupied by Frederick William Ashby. Subtler alterations are the replacement of the gas lamps with brighter modern electric street lights and the lack of the ubiquitous parked cars of today. Now a back street, Church Street was still the main road to Wraysbury at this time, the present Wraysbury Road dating to the 1960s, but the only vehicles visible here are two bicycles and a delivery waggon.

ST. MARY'S CHURCH LADS' BRIGADE BAND 1926

After several unsuccessful attempts during the late 1890s, a Church Lads' Brigade for St. Mary's Parish was finally started on Monday, 19th February, 1900. The objects of this body were to train the boys in "attachment to our Lord and His Church, and promote among them habits of reverence, obedience, self control, and all that tends towards Christian manliness", by a combination of Bible classes, etc., military organisation and drill. To this end, funds were sought for the purchase of rifles and slings for drilling, and these were received on 15th August. The Brigade's first Captain was a former Volunteer, Mr. R. Tims. The lads paid for their own outfits — a forage cap, fatigue cap, belt and haversack, costing 3s. 3½ d. Initially, numbers were limited to 30 through lack of space for drilling. A drum and fife band of 14 members was considered highly desirable, but this could not be started for some years for lack of someone to instruct them and the £6-£7 required to purchase instruments.

ST. MARY'S CHURCH, 1895 and c.1905

Staines has had a Parish Church on or near this site since at least 1179 and probably earlier. By 1826, however, the old church was considered too small for the growing population of the town and was in very bad repair. One Sunday, during an evening service, the window and at least 14 ft. of the wall of the north "transept" collapsed half-way through the sermon. Fortunately nobody was killed, as it was a wet evening with high winds and the newspaper reported that "the congregation were not very numerous, consisting of probably between 200 and 300 persons." It was decided that the whole church would have to be rebuilt except for the tower. A private Act of Parliament was obtained, enabling Trustees to build a new church with the help of a £250 grant from the Church Building Society. It was designed by J.B. Watson in Gothic style and constructed of yellow stock brick with a castellated parapet around the slate roof. The tower windows were enlarged and its height raised by the addition of the pinnacles shown here, which were removed in 1947 following bomb damage during the last war. The building, intended to hold 1,000 people and costing £3,000, was consecrated in 1829. The interior view shows the church after the addition of the eastern apse and before the removal of the old box pews and the old ceiling in 1899. One of the three windows in the chancel was presented by the Emperor Frederick III of Germany in memory of his children's nanny, Miss Augusta Byng, who lived in Binbury Row.

CHURCH COTTAGE c.1903

The part of Church Street between the Bell Inn and the Lammas was formerly known as Binbury Row or Binbury Street. The name Binbury was in use by 1336, when it seems to have referred to the higher ground around the Church – at that time a populous area. In 1874 Church Cottage was occupied by Mrs. Jane Elliott, who ran a ladies' school there, and by 1882 the work was shared with her daughter Frances. At the time of this photograph Frances was advertising her services as a music teacher, while her sister Mary Jane had taken over the running of the school. Small private schools of this type were considered a genteel way for single or widowed women to support themselves. The sisters carried on until the 1920s, Miss M.J. Elliott still being resident in the cottage in 1930.

CHURCH ISLAND c.1920

The sheltered backwater between the Middlesex bank and Church Island provided facilities for river-based sport for many years up to the late 1920s. Apart from the ad-hoc fishing by small boys with home-made rods, the area was home to the members of Staines Swimming Club, whose headquarters were on the upstream end of the island. John Tims' boatyard, from which it was possible to hire the variety of sculled craft in the foreground, gave up here c.1928, although their larger premises below the railway bridge carried on building and letting river craft. The creek was also home to the annual jollification which surrounded the Staines and Egham Juvenile Regatta. This, inaugurated in 1906, was usually held on the first Thursday in August until 1931. Leisure use of the island itself is indicated by the bungalow development, which seems to date from this peak period of Staines' rôle as a resort centre.

THE LONDON STONE c.1910

The ancient stone for which Staines was long famed originally stood just up-stream of the old Staines Bridge. It was placed there in 1280, on the pedestal shown here, to mark the westernmost jurisdiction of the City of London and was moved further from the river in 1619. When the present Staines Bridge was built in 1832, the stone was moved to the position shown here, at the Lammas. As shown, it was easily visible from the river, but in September 1931 the Clerk to the Council wrote to the Thames Conservancy about "a considerable increase in the size of a piece of land between the London Stone and the main river." This was thought to be caused mainly by the owners of small bungalows downstream, who had increased the size of their land by depositing material in the river, causing an eddy at the outlet of the Shire Ditch. In 1986 the badly eroded stone was removed to Staines Library and replaced with a replica. It now (1999) stands in the Old Town Hall.

THE LAMMAS c.1935

In 1899 the press reported a spate of prosecutions by the Thames Conservancy of those bathing "improperly dressed". They considered "boating costume" the appropriate apparel for swimmers. By 1915 the Staines & Egham Swimming Club boasted its own changing facilities, but the local Council were concerned at the lack of similar provision for the general public. Their chosen spot was on Staines Moor rather than the Thames, but the estimated cost of dressing sheds and necessary dredging was c.£100, which could not be justified in time of war. In January 1922 John Ashby gave 15½ acres of the Lammas to the town for a recreation ground and the Commoners donated £1,200 for the provision of a safe bathing place and to prepare the land for its new use. Staines U.D.C. responded with plans for a brick bathing place and tennis courts. By 1936, they were considering building a swimming pool in Bridge Street, but the scheme was abandoned and local people continued to bathe in the river.

STAINES FOOTBALL CLUB 1903-4

Staines Football Club had taken part in the Surrey Cup in the early 1880s. They were winners in the West London Alliance (Div. 1) in 1900, the West London League (Div. 1) in 1901 and the Middlesex Junior Cup in 1902 and again in 1904 when they were also Runners-up to Staines Town F.C. in the West Middlesex League. They celebrated their success with this photograph taken in a local studio. In April 1910, however, the "Middlesex Chronicle" regretfully remarked that "After their success in cup engagements Staines have sadly disappointed their supporters in League matches." Their ground seems to have been at the Lammas. The Club members shown here are:

Back: W. Sylvester, H. Swan, W. Langdon, E. Lines, W. Chilton.
Second Row: R. Howard, H. Pratley, H. Tanner, A. Reed, A. Nickolas, H. Mussard, P.E. Lloyd (Hon. Sec.)
Third Row: R. Walmsley (Capt.), A. Rickard, A. Ellis (Vice-Capt.), E. Bavin.
Front: E. Bolton, A. Hawthorne, C. Prestoe, A. Moseley, A. Coates.

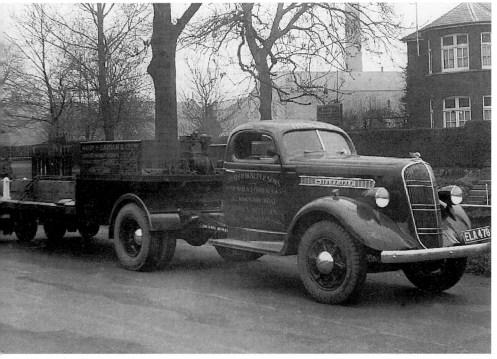

HUXLEY'S LOW-LOADER
c.1937

Three local businesses are represented in this photograph, showing a 1936 American Studebaker low-loader outside the G.W.R. Station in Moor Lane. The vehicle belonged to the firm of Joseph Huxley and Sons, haulage contractors. This company originated in St Arvans, Monmouthshire, and came to Staines in 1926 and by the time of their 50th anniversary in 1976 they had a fleet of 40 vehicles. Huxley's were on contract to the engineering company Harry H. Gardam & Co. Ltd., of Church Street, founded in 1905, whose name can be seen on the trailer. They specialised in large second-hand equipment, normally transported by train. In earlier years such items were taken to the station by Gardam's own steam traction engine, but Huxley's, who had a yard in Church Street and the latest haulage vehicles as shown here, proved a very convenient alternative. In the background, to the left of the station building, part of the linoleum factory is visible.

SIGNAL BOX, STAINES WEST STATION, c.1906

Before the introduction of modern technology, every station and junction on the railway required its own signal box. The signalman commanded a degree of respect as a skilled worker responsible for the safe running of that portion of the railway under his control. Great pride was taken in keeping the signal box spotlessly clean and the brass gleaming. Controls were handled with a duster to avoid unsightly and corrosive fingerprints. The box shown here seems to have stood just outside the station between the railway line and the Wyrardisbury River. Maps indicate, however, that by 1934 the position of this vital facility had been moved to a point a little further south, between the goods yard and the line leading into the station.

STAINES WEST STATION c.1930

In 1885 the Staines and West Drayton Railway opened its line to Staines, using this terminus in Moor Lane. The station building was unusual in having been converted from a private house built in 1820 for Charles Finch, owner of the adjacent Mustard Mill. The platforms were constructed in what had been the front garden. This picture, taken from the top of the brewery tower, shows a considerable quantity of goods traffic in the yard. The station forecourt became a bus terminus. The goods yard and adjoining platforms were replaced in the 1960s by a heating-oil terminal which continued to use the station after passenger services ceased in 1965. By 1977, when it was listed by the Department of the Environment as a building of historic interest, the station building was derelict. It was sold to Spelthorne Borough Council for £1 and in 1981-82 it was converted into prestige offices. The columns which supported the platform canopy are now utilised as lamp standards.

CLUB HOUSE, RUNNYMEDE RANGES c.1910

There were rifle butts on the slopes of Coopers Hill, Runnymede, Egham, in the latter half of the 19th century. In 1891 these were superseded by a new and more comprehensive range at Yeoveney. The new ranges were constructed for the benefit of the volunteer force by the Metropolitan Rifle Range Co. Ltd. and officially opened in 1892. Another earlier range on Staines Moor, opened in 1862 for the 44th Middlesex Rifle Volunteer Corps, closed in 1892 following a petition to the War Office by the Staines & West Drayton Railway, who were concerned for the safety of their passengers. By 1902 there were some 100 targets with ranges from 100 to 1,200 yards, a revolver range, camping ground, canteen and the pavilion or club house shown here. The range was offered for sale in December 1920 and subsequently fell into disuse.

YEOVENEY HALT, 1st October, 1961

The G.W.R. originally opened this small station on its Staines to West Drayton line in 1895 in order to transport soldiers to and from the Runnymede Range, three minutes' walk away. It was known originally as "Runemede Range", but later as "Yeoveney Halt". By the early 1930s the range was disused, but the halt at Yeoveney continued to serve local residents until the closure of the line in March 1965. Those wishing to avail themselves of the service had to hail their train by sticking out a hand, as when catching a bus. The photograph shows the diesel railcar which by this time operated the push-pull service on this little branch line to West Drayton.

FUND-RAISING 1910

The Staines Nurse Society appointed its first nurse, Nurse Woodlock, in 1891. Charity football matches, commonly in fancy dress, were a popular method of raising money and the event advertised here took place in the Linoleum Meadow on Thursday, April 7th, 1910. With shops open until 8.00 or 10.00 p.m. on other days, and Sundays sacrosanct, early closing day was the only opportunity for staff to enjoy football. In this case, the local team was recruited by the local Postmaster, Mr. W. Herbert Bartlett, on behalf of Staines Athletic Association and defeated the 2nd Scots Guards by 2 goals to 1. His team was composed of Higgs, Bryan & Palmer, R. Young, Davis & Brown, Tidbury, Morris, McDermott, F. Young and Bridger. Sadly, no first names are recorded. The match was followed by tea at the White Lion and a smoking concert. Miss Toombs and Miss Bullock, dressed as Red Cross Nurses, raised a considerable sum for the Fund, assisted by Mr. Stent with the barrel organ.

MILL MEAD 1935

The Silver Jubilee of King George V was celebrated locally with enthusiastic patriotism. The main festivities were preceded by a Jubilee Air Display at Hythe End Farm on 23rd April. Events on the Ashby Recreation Ground on Monday, 3rd May, commenced at 10 a.m. with a short religious service, followed by children's sports, after which they were entertained to tea in a huge marquee. There was much cheering, "especially when the chocolate was distributed." The "christening" of the new fire engine and the presentation of prizes preceded floodlit dancing, Scouts' sports, concert and lighting of a beacon. The Old People's Dinner at the Town Hall was held on Wednesday and a Thanksgiving Service on Sunday. Public and private buildings were decorated, the Majestic Cinema and an illuminated crown surmounting the brewery being especially noted. The residents of Mill Mead and Fairfield Terrace were singled out for "A most praise-worthy effort in the matter of street decoration" and "expressed a desire that a pictorial record should be made of their demonstration of loyalty."

HALE MILL c.1890

A mill was in existence on this site on the River Colne in the 13th century and during the reign of Edward I part of it was the property of John le Hale, from whom its name is presumably derived. By 1755 it belonged to John Finch, owner of Pound Mill, and remained in his family's possession for the next 109 years, although by 1826 they no longer worked it themselves. At that date, and until at least 1843, it was occupied by William Murrell, miller and mealman. It was in use as a papier maché works c.1855 and it is said to have been used at one time as a calico printing works. This may have involved the use of large water-powered rollers which would have been a valuable asset for Frederick Walton when he came to Hale Mill in 1864 to establish his pioneering linoleum factory. The company bought the mill outright in 1871.

THE LINOLEUM FACTORY c.1950
and CORK STORE c.1910

Frederick Walton was an engineer from Yorkshire who invented the new floor covering which he eventually named "linoleum". It was originally a mixture of oxidised linseed oil and resins with ground cork, pressed on to hessian. The photograph shows the process of creating patterned linoleum by carefully arranging cut linoleum shapes on the hessian before it passed through the rollers which bonded it together. Precision was vital and the workers were not permitted to talk or sing as they worked. Their working day in 1938 was from 8 a.m. to 5.30 p.m., for which they received 14s. (70p) per week. The large quantities of cork and resins on the premises naturally represented a fire hazard, and serious fires did occur at the factory, which wisely always maintained its own fire engine with a trained crew. One such occasion was in April 1914, when fire broke out in the linoleum-drying rooms at about 9 a.m. and spread to adjoining stores stacked with sacks of cork dust. The Company's fire brigade, with the help of the Staines Brigade, took three hours to extinguish the blaze, which caused £8,000 worth of damage, including the loss of some eight miles of linoleum. Men are shown here loading bales of cork in the sheds where it was stored before milling in the hammer mills to reduce it to dust.

HIGH STREET/CLARENCE STREET JUNCTION c.1910

The gas lamps used by traders to illuminate their shop fronts were of particular value in winter, when the inadequacies of the street lights were most keenly felt. That on the left adorns Swann's chemist's shop on the corner of Thames Street, while others can be seen on the premises of Ellis & Co., grocers, and on The Cabin beerhouse on the right. On the corners of Clarence Street are the imposing façades of William Eves, oil and colour man, and Mr. Perkins. Francis Perkins had established himself as a butcher in Church Street c.1850 and the family business grew steadily. By 1903 George James Perkins was trading as a butcher from 5, Church Street and 5, Clarence Street; a pork butcher at 4, High Street; a fishmonger at 7, Clarence Street; and a fruiterer at 2, High Street. His Clarence Street premises were altered and improved in 1904, re-opening in April. This was the first shop in Staines with electric lighting. The first-floor conservatory was added at this time.

MARKET SQUARE 1906

No doubt taking a professional interest in the recording of this event, the Captain of the Staines Fire Brigade, Ralph Lane, was a photographer at 54, High Street. The Staines Brigade and those of neighbouring towns had turned out to "christen" a new fire engine (see page 63) and gathered in front of the Town Hall. This must have been quite literally a dazzling event, with the parade turn-out of highly-polished helmets and accoutrements, brass-bound engines and equally highly finished musical instruments. In the background, adjacent to the Town Hall steps, can be seen the local Brigade's treasured possession, its manual engine of 1738. This was normally stored in a lean-to shelter behind the fire station until 1921, when it was transferred to a new shelter in the Memorial Gardens. It is still to be seen in Spelthorne Museum.

20

FIRE ENGINE 1926

Following a decision of the Staines Urban District Council in March 1926 that a Dennis motor fire engine be purchased, a new machine was duly delivered from Guildford on 17th May, 1926. This 25 h.p. appliance was acquired in response to the old "steamer" being found defective and although the engine cost £799, the Council decided against spending another £200 on a larger 40 h.p. model of a similar pumping capacity. The Dennis company was one of the leading manufacturers of motorised fire appliances and was reported at the time as having received orders for 70 of this type. Arrangements were made to celebrate its arrival with a "christening" ceremony, which was carried out on 3rd June by the wife of Chief Officer Capt. T. Crimble. Mrs. Crimble named the machine "George V". As with earlier machines, the festivities were attended by neighbouring brigades, who entertained the crowds with a display of water jets. In 1935 a Leyland vehicle was purchased and the "George V" was passed to the Ashford Brigade.

WAR MEMORIAL c.1925

The First World War had a great impact here, as elsewhere. The number of men from the Linoleum Factory alone who had joined the Armed Forces was 673: of these, 83 were killed and 453 returned to the factory. The Town Hall Gardens, with additional land given by Councillor John Drake, were laid out as a Memorial Garden and money was raised by public subscription for a monument. The War Memorial, shown here, was executed by Messrs. Goodale & Co., monumental masons, of 72, High Street, to a design by Mr. E.J. Barrett, the town Surveyor. It is of Portland stone, with the names of the 196 fallen inscribed on the central block and flanked by figures representing a soldier, a sailor, an airman and a marine, under the cross of sacrifice. Above is the Angel of Peace holding the Torch of Freedom and a Wreath of Victory. It was unveiled by Brigadier General the Earl of Lucan, K.C.B., on Sunday, 19th December, 1920, following a Service of Remembrance in the Town Hall.

THE BLUE ANCHOR 1913

The elegant elevation of the Blue Anchor Inn is a rebuild c.1700 of a much older structure and contains many contemporary architectural details. Listed as being of special architectural interest, its frontage still includes five "blind" windows reputedly infilled during the imposition of the Window Tax in force 1695-1811. Its ground-floor symmetry at the time of the photograph was somewhat altered by the use of the left-hand side of the property – no. 15, High Street – as a separate shop. The landlord at this time, Ted Glue, had held the licence since 1903, having moved from the Nag's Head, Egham, where his name led to the soubriquet of "The Glue Pot".

VICTORY PARADE, 11th May, 1945

Following the conclusion of the War in Europe, the first Sunday after V.E. Day was the occasion for Staines' own Victory Parade. The participants marched via Kingston Road into the Market Square, headed by the band of the 1st Middx. Battn. of the Home Guard, with members of the crew of Staines' "own" submarine H.M.S. Unshaken, who were guests of the town for the weekend. Other bodies involved in the ceremony included: a Royal Naval Unit, Royal Naval Old Comrades' Association, Army units including a tank, the A.T.S., Home Guard, Army Cadets, Old Contemptibles, British Legion, R.A.F. Unit 398 Squadron A.T.C. with trumpet band, all branches of the Civil Defence services, W.V.S., Women's Land Army, S.J.A.B., British Red Cross, Voluntary Nursing Unit, Sea Scouts, Boy Scouts and Boys' Brigade. The meeting, commencing at 3.30 p.m., was addressed by Mr. W.H. Walter, J.P., Chairman of the Staines Urban District Council.

MARKET SQUARE c.1955

This evocative image of a bustling Staines Market was taken from the convenient vantage point of the Town Hall. In fact, the town's market has undergone varying fortunes over the years, but was certainly in existence by 1218, when the Sheriff of Middlesex was ordered to see that Staines Market was held on Friday rather than Sunday. The importance of the facility was sufficient for the erection by 1662 of a permanent market house which stood to the left of the present Town Hall site. The market declined in the 19th century and was discontinued by 1862. However, the Act which permitted the building of the Town Hall also allowed for the re-establishment of a regular market. Although photographs taken at the end of the 19th century show a very desultory array of goods on offer, by 1933 a greengrocer at 5, High Street, facing the site, reported Saturday evening to be the busiest time and over 4,000 customers during the day!

MARKET SQUARE c.1959

Familiar to generations of television viewers as the personal transport of "Doctor Who", the blue police box as seen here in the Market Square was, in fact, a vital part of the Metropolitan Police Force's communication network. First introduced in the mid-1930s, the Staines box was sited here in 1936, when the local newspapers advised readers that the system could be used free of charge for any purpose affecting police work. As well as giving members of the public a dedicated phone line to the services of the police force, the boxes allowed privacy and shelter for constables signing on and off duty and a place to sit and eat sandwiches after beat duties. Also seen adjacent to the box is the pillar which supported the air-raid warning siren. This, introduced in anticipation of the Second World War, was also part of a comprehensive system which could provide flood warnings to residents and, as part of the continuing post-war civil defence strategy, give notice of a nuclear attack.

HIGH STREET c.1865

This early view shows an impressive array of mid-Victorian shop-fronts, a circumstance which belies the fact that much of the High Street was residential. On the extreme left, the premises with the large clock above the window belonged to J. Goring & Son, butchers, who traded here from 1790 to the 1960s. Goring Square, on the site of their slaughter house, is named after them. The Blue Anchor was run in 1867 by Mrs. Charlotte Piggott, with the small shop on the left of the ground floor occupied by Thomas William Stephens, auctioneer and appraiser, who had been in business since the 1840s. George New, the greengrocer, whose shop is just visible on the extreme right, had started his business c.1860, and it seems to have lasted only about ten years. The apparent emptiness of the street reflects the long exposures required at this time, as the inclusion of passing vehicles or pedestrians would have caused a blurred image.

MARKET SQUARE c.1905

The annual running of the Ascot races seems to have benefited many residents of the town. As a natural stopping point en route or on the return to Town after a day at the races, Staines' many licensed premises profited from the free-spending trippers. The coaches and brakes seen passing the square may also have obliged the local children who called for coppers to be thrown to them. The Ascot traffic in 1904 is reported as furnishing a severe test for a new road dust preventer under trial, called Pyne Oiline, the Council Surveyor considering the effect very good. Another indication of the prevalent road conditions is the large, moveable, curved standpipe adjacent to the horse trough. This was used to fill the Council's water carts for the purpose of dust laying in the district. Dust was a constant cause of complaint in the summer and in 1907, although the town's main roads were being tar-dressed, the Chamber of Commerce complained that the dust was now black! The granite trough, which served to water cattle and horses, also incorporated a drinking fountain and had been erected at a cost of £130 raised by public subscription in 1883.

TESCO, 6-8 HIGH STREET, c.1959

The firm which trades as Tesco had its origins in the grocery business established in 1919 by Jacob "Jack" Cohen in London's East End. The familiar company name came about as a result of a deal with T.E. Stockwell, a tea importer, in 1924 and is an amalgamation of his initials and Cohen's surname. Expanding first in the London area, by the mid-1930s the company had over 40 sites. Many of these were in indoor market premises with the familiar motto of "Pile it high, sell it cheap". Tesco's came to Staines some time in the mid-1930s, with premises at no. 2, High Street, eventually occupying 2-8, High Street, and after the war had begun the move to self-service and supermarket trading. Even this relatively large site was given up in the 1980s and Tesco's eventually moved to a new site at Ashford.

STAINES MARKET c.1959

Originally taken for town planning purposes by Staines Urban District Council, this photographic record captured more of the town's once-familiar retail scene. The imposing elevation of Staines Market dated from the mid-1930s, when similar arcade premises opened around the country in suitable locations. The Staines building is also said to have had a snooker hall on its first floor before the last war. As seen here, the market was principally occupied by the Tesco emporium, although footwear and children's clothing retailers were also housed here. As with many other areas of the town's core shopping area, the street scene then and now presents a fascinating mixture of ancient and modern façades. The properties commencing at no. 1, Church Street and housing Sewmaster, etc., are in fact of Cromwellian origin. Their one-time neighbour at 2, High Street was one of Staines' many historic inns, The George. Although this was demolished in the 19th century, following demolition of the "Staines Market" building in 1995, the new licensed premises occupying the site are also called "The George".

W.H. SMITH & SON 1934

W.H. Smith had had a bookstall at Staines Junction Station since the mid-19th century (See p. 50). In 1905 the company decided to open shops in place of some of their former bookstalls, and the emphasis of their business progressively shifted towards this form of trading. They opened their Staines branch at 49, High Street, in 1934 and the photograph shows the shop soon afterwards. The premises had formerly been occupied by the draper, G. Betts, and the company purchased the goodwill of J.L. Gubbins, bookseller, newsagent and stationer, of 36, High Street. This enterprise included a circulating library which had been in operation since at least 1902 and can be seen advertised to the right of the shop window. In 1971 the branch was expanded to its present size by the acquisition of no. 51, previously occupied by W. Hinds, jewellers, and before that by the Midland Bank, which had moved to its present site at nos. 61-63 in the 1950s.

GOODMAN PLACE 1961

Typical of many towns, Staines has numerous ancient passages and rights of way which reflect the continuity of boundaries and building plots. Staines' Roman origins are now well known, but this now-vanished aspect adjacent to the High Street also provides an interesting reminder of the antiquity of the current topography. The gentle slope of the lane neatly illustrates the fact that the original settlement area used the highest parts of the land available, with the High Street and other heavily-utilised areas dependent on the underlying gravel contours to avoid flooding. The name of the lane, originally a cul-de-sac leading to the Friends' Meeting House, is of modern origin referring to the adjacent High Street frontage of Morford & Goodman's shop. William Wreyford Goodman, who came to the area c.1880, was a one-time Chairman of the local Chamber of Commerce and died in 1921.

FRIENDS' BURIAL GROUND 1976

Although as relatively recently as 1953 a history of Middlesex by Michael Robbins could state that "no remains indicating Roman settlement have been found there", work in Staines in the last 30 years has demonstrated the enormous potential of the town. In fact, there have been numerous reports of the finding of recognisably Roman objects in the area from the 19th century onwards and historical references and "stray finds" in the vicinity led to the inescapable conclusion that Staines was the site of the Roman settlement of Pontes. The first archaeological excavation in the town took place in 1969 when during the redevelopment of the Barclay's Bank site, Mrs. Maureen Rendell, working for the London Museum and aided by members of the Egham-by-Runnymede Historical Society, recovered remarkable evidence of Roman military and civilian occupation. Following these discoveries, opportunities to excavate in the town were seized in advance of the increasing number of redevelopments, and in particular the Central Area Development, which opened up large areas of the High Street and backland sites for investigation. The Friends' Burial Ground, seen under excavation here, produced detailed evidence of not only Roman but also prehistoric occupation in the heart of the town. Although the site was heavily cut by burial plots, careful excavation of it also revealed dramatic evidence of the series of floods which have so affected the various phases of occupation here over the last 6,000 years.

FRIENDS' MEETING HOUSE c.1930

The second meeting house of the Staines Religious Society of Friends (commonly known as Quakers) was opened on 18th July, 1844. The building, to a design of Samuel Danvers, was on part of a substantial plot to the rear of 55, High Street, originally purchased by the Friends in 1840. On excavation in 1975-76, the Meeting House was found to have had substantial foundations of concrete and an internal brick-lined well. The property was also the site of the Staines Friends' later burial ground, which contained the mortal remains of 82 Friends interred here between 1848 and 1949. In 1936 the building seen here was demolished, although a wooden hut erected in the grounds in 1937 served the Staines Meeting until 1975, when the central area redevelopment scheme cleared the site. The human remains were transferd to the Friends' burial ground at Jordans in Buckinghamshire and the Meeting moved to Egham, where it continues to worship.

HIGH STREET c.1947

The photograph shows clearly the unusual width of this part of the High Street. From before 1754 until 1802, a group of buildings known as the Middle Row stood in the centre of the road here, possibly permanent market stalls, suggesting that the weekly market reached beyond the stretch of road nearest the Thames. The twice-yearly local fairs continued here until their abolition in 1896 and contemporary photographs show a variety of rides and attractions erected on the south side of the street. This core area has thus benefited from the persistence of the ancient building line, creating a suitable space for part of the new pedestrian precinct. Although Staines had recently experienced its share of war-time damage the High Street was untouched by the bombing. The building boom of the 1930s which gave the street many of the now-familiar elevations had not yet resumed, but in 1957 the Crown and Anchor public house, in the left foreground, an Edwardian rebuild of a much older structure, was demolished.

POST OFFICE c.1910

Now 100 years old, these premises are currently a McDonald's Restaurant, part of the multi-national chain which began near Pasadena, U.S.A., in 1937 and opened its first UK restaurant at Woolwich in 1974. In 1898 Westbourne House, an imposing three-storey residence on the site previously occupied by Mr. Ashby, a member of the local banking family, was acquired by Mr. Charles Reeves, butcher. He demolished the house and built a block of three shops. He moved into the present no. 56 in 1902, while in 1899 no. 62, shown here, became the main Post Office, which had formerly been on the other side of the road. At about midnight on Tuesday, 5th August, 1914, a big crowd outside the Post Office cheered heartily at the news, announced by Mr. Kind, chief of the telegraphic staff, that war had broken out. They then paraded through the town singing patriotic songs. The present Post Office opened in 1931 and these premises were occupied by various retail businesses until McDonald's moved in.

INTERNATIONAL STORES c.1905

This ubiquitous chain of grocer's shops was well established by 1910, with branches all over the South of England. Their familiar signage in gold and black was a feature of many High Streets. The Staines branch had opened in the 1890s at 40, High Street, on the site of the later Halford's. As the photograph indicates, the Stores employed a considerable number of staff, ranging from the Manager to the drivers and errand boys who would have delivered groceries to customers' houses. Tea was on offer from 1s. 4d. (7p) per quarter and choicest butter at one shilling (5p) per pound. With many school leavers earning 10 s. (50p) per week, and older workers often only £2, many housewives had to budget very carefully. Hours were long – 8 a.m.-8 p.m. Monday to Wednesday, late opening on Friday and Saturday until 9 p.m. and 10 p.m. respectively and early closing at 1 p.m. on Thursday.

FIRST STAINES (ST. MARY'S) SCOUTS c.1924

The First Staines troop of scouts were unusual in having a woman, Miss May Rhodes, as Assistant Scoutmaster. She played piano and flute, and she and her sister both played in the London Philharmonic and Symphonic Orchestras. Mr. Ede was the Group Scoutmaster for many years and the Cubmaster about this time was Mr. V. Cobb. The scouts and wolf cubs are shown here marching past nos. 63-67, High Street, site of the present Midland (HSBC) and NatWest banks. On the extreme left is part of M. & H.J. Ashby's wine & spirit merchants. No. 67 was occupied in 1922 by Dale & Newbery, solicitors, and next door, Madame Idé, gown manufacturer, had a shop for a short time, whilst Frederick Cherry, optician, occupied the first floor. No. 63, C. Clinch's fruiterer's, was rebuilt in 1927 as Dexter's Café (see below). To its right are Mr. Dexter's earlier premises.

63, HIGH STREET c.1935

Lewis Dexter served his apprenticeship as a baker with Mr. Tolley of 47-49, Church Street, and in 1905 took over the business. Soon afterwards he acquired 55 (now 61), High Street (see above) and in the 1920s, after his eldest son joined him in the business, he sold the Church Street business to W.J. Frisby. These premises, next door, were built for him in 1927 and he diversified into catering, while the bakery moved to 45, High Street. In August 1958 the business moved to no. 17, where it remained, run latterly by Tower Bakeries Ltd., until the shop was redeveloped in 1986. The figure above the door, popularly known as "the golden boy" but properly the "Daughter of the Goddess of Fame", was gracing the High Street by the 1890s, over the shop of Mr. Rogers the builder at no. 55. Many residents remember it above the premises at no. 17 and later outside the Age Concern Day Centre. In 1996 Spelthorne Council moved it to the Walled Garden, Sunbury, from which it was subsequently stolen.

ELMSLEIGH HOUSE c.1910

This Victorian villa, dating to c.1878, was situated south of the High Street behind the present Barclay's Bank. From the 1870s until 1888 it was occupied by Morris Ashby, junior (1847-1906), one of the Staines family who once dominated much of the town's business and social life. His father, Morris Ashby, senior, and uncle, Henry John, ran a wine merchant's business in the High Street. He was followed by Osmond F. Giddy and, by 1902, Arthur Carpenter. Later residents included Mr. Henry Bergh in the 1930s. In 1952 the Staines Urban District Council took Elmsleigh over to accommodate its Clerk's Department and it remained in the hands of the local authority until its demolition in 1974 to make way for the new Elmsleigh Centre, which opened on 22nd February, 1980. The site of the house and part of its grounds was excavated in 1974-75, producing evidence of occupation from the third century A.D., with a Roman roadway running across the northern part of the site.

HIGH STREET c.1936

Keen eyes will spot the very early use of the belisha beacon as an aid to allow pedestrians to cross the normally busy main road. These devices were named after the then Minister of Transport, Leslie Hore-Belisha (1893-1957), as part of the response to the alarming incidence of road traffic deaths. Also prominent in the street scene were the premises of the house furnishers, John Perring. This enterprise was originally founded in the late 19th century by Henry Perring in London's furniture centre of Tottenham Court Road. His sons, John and William, opened a series of retail premises-that in Staines, originally at 58, High Street, by 1914. By 1922, following renumbering of the street c. 1920, this three-storey art deco emporium had been opened as nos. 64-66. During the last war its premises housed part of the Perring's war effort, producing armature coils, of which a total of 8½ million were made by the all-female work-force at the various branches involved.

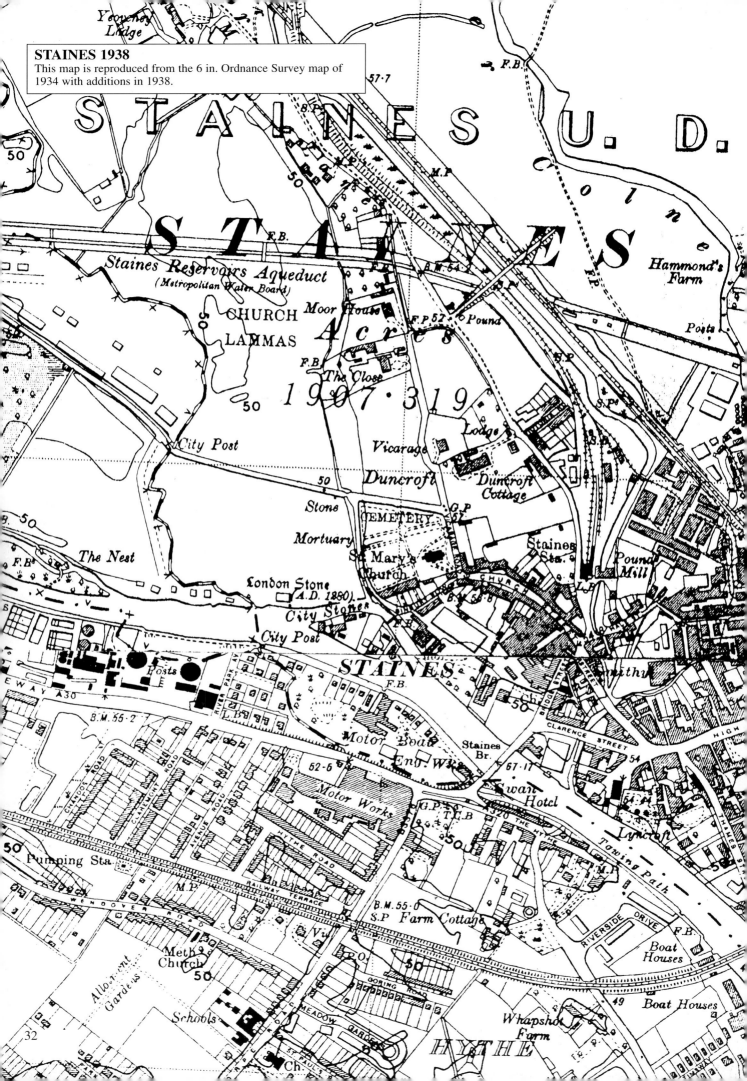

STAINES 1938
This map is reproduced from the 6 in. Ordnance Survey map of 1934 with additions in 1938.

93, HIGH STREET c.1912

One hundred years ago, when it was estimated that the population of Staines parish was c.6,500, the High Street alone had four grocers plus numerous other specialist food retailers. This handsome castellated façade was home to one of the growing number of such enterprises. William Henry Pledger's business seems to have been established c.1910 and was a typical family-run grocer's which served the local community. Intense competition between the small retailers and the growing chains (see P. 29) meant that contemporary shoppers could be influenced by price variations of a fraction of a penny. Mr. Pledger seems to have departed soon after 1930 and the premises were then used by Dunn & Co., the gentlemen's outfitters. It is now (1999) a Vodafone shop

HIGH STREET c.1920

Looking west along the High Street, the vista still ended at this date with Waine's china shop (previously Swann's chemist's), on the far corner of Thames Street: above it can be seen the clock tower of the Town Hall. In the extreme left foreground is part of the shop front of George Bone's tobacconist's at 95, High Street. Pledger's shop (see above) is just beyond this, at the near end of a block of four retail premises of which only two now remain (1999). On the right, the proprietors of Herbert and Herbert have taken advantage of their location on the corner of Norris Road by using the end wall to advertise their hairdressing salon, while a large banner projecting above the High Street proclaims their photographic stock. Nearer the camera is the jeweller's shop of Benjamin Luther Virgo. In 1914 Mr. Virgo lent the rooms above his shop to the Staines Brotherhood, who furnished them for the accommodation of Belgian Refugees. Virgo's remained in business into the 1970s.

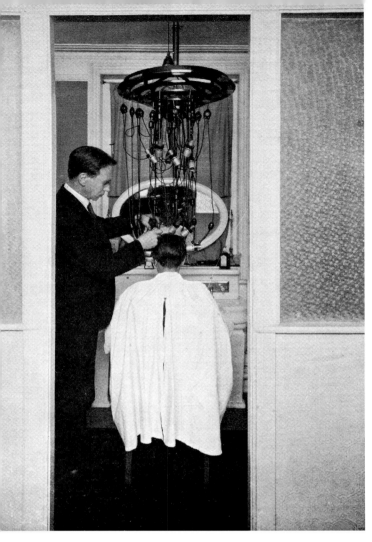

HERBERT & HERBERT 1930

Henry W. Herbert opened his chemist's shop at 62 (later 70), High Street, c.1900, having already established himself in Egham. In 1906 this was one of five shops in Staines selling photographic equipment, and of four equipped with a darkroom. Cine films were also advertised in 1930. A local girl who went to work for Mr. Herbert's family on leaving school in the 1920s later recalled that Mrs. Herbert used to go to the shop to "do the books". By 1930 the proprietors, now Herbert & Herbert, had built up a large business which included toiletries, dog and cat medicines, garden chemicals and nursery requisites. Messrs. Herbert advertised that they dispensed all medicines personally. Medicines were delivered (to those who could afford them), mainly by bicycle, at intervals during the day and, if urgently needed, a special messenger would be sent at no extra charge. Above the chemist's shop were hairdressing salons, including cubicles such as that illustrated, offering the latest permanent-waving technology. The shop was demolished in October 1958.

101-107 HIGH STREET 1933

Another of the leading names in the commercial life of Staines was the Bone family, who were involved in numerous enterprises in the town. The photograph was taken in advance of the redevelopment of this block of property for Marks & Spencer's and F.W. Woolworth's new premises. It gives a fascinating, if somewhat alarming, view of the days when motor spirit could be stored and dispensed in town centres. Previously occupied by William Carpenter's extensive coach and motor body works, by 1933 the site was in multiple occupation. Nos. 101-103, High Street, the right-hand side of the large block, were demolished in November 1933 for the building of what was described as a "superstore" for Woolworth's. These premises were acquired by Mr. G. Bone c.1878 and during the demolition fireplaces, panelling and other architectural features from what was thought to be a 15th century building were recovered. Bone's garage at no. 97, High Street was also rebuilt shortly after this and by 1937 the firm, who were also undertakers, had further premises in Thames Street.

MARKS & SPENCER April 1933 and 1959

Originating in the "Penny Bazaar" market stall started in Leeds by Michael Marks in 1884, the firm of Marks & Spencer had by 1914 grown into a chain of 140 stores with additional warehouses in Birmingham and London. They became a public limited company in 1926 and registered the St. Michael trademark in 1928. The new purpose-built branch in Staines opened on 19th May, 1933. The building, completed in 11 weeks, had a floor space of 130 feet by 42 feet, with walls panelled in mahogany and a white tiled canteen for 40 girl employees where a good meal could be bought for 6d (2½ p). This may reflect the fact that the company established its Staff Welfare Department in the same year. The new store boasted 20 departments and was now one of over 160 branches throughout the country. The first manager was Mr. A.P. Smyth. Since 1933, the store has been extended and modernised many times, notably in 1959 and in the late 1970s. The interior view shows the store on 13th March, 1959, just after completion of the work.

WOOLWORTH'S LADIES' FOOTBALL TEAM c.1934

On Thursday, 2nd November, 1933, under the auspices of the Staines Bonfire Society, the first of several football matches between the ladies of F.W. Woolworth and the newly-arrived firm of Marks & Spencer was played on the Staines Linoleum Football Ground. In that year, Marks & Spencer's team won 5-0. This photograph is thought to show the team of 1934, when Woolworth's were said to have shown some "sparkling form", culminating in a 1-1 draw after extra time, each team holding the "Empire" Challenge Cup, presented by the Directors of the New Empire Cinema, for six months. Arthur Rowe, of Tottenham Hotspur, kicked off for Marks & Spencer in front of a very large crowd. Proceeds were used to furnish the massage room at the Cottage Hospital and for a portable service and dressing station for the 123rd (Staines) Division of the St. John Ambulance Brigade. The 1934 team were: M. R. Coles; F. Henson & D. Phillips; E. Ellis, I. Woodcock & D. Phillips; C. Sheffield, B. Lemon, I. Hawthorne (capt.), N. Clark & D. Stratton.

THE WHITE LION c.1935

In the left foreground is perhaps the most lamented vanished building in Staines, the White Lion public house. This old timber-framed inn was in existence certainly in 1612 and probably in the mid-16th century, although most of the black-stained timbering here was a recent addition for purely aesthetic purposes. The landlord at this time was Mr. Ernest Newport. The building, together with the shops between it and the railway bridge, had the misfortune to stand in the narrowest part of the High Street, as is clearly shown in this photograph. This made it a prominent landmark, visible from a considerable distance along the street – but it also marked it out as a problem for those endeavouring to cure the town's severe traffic congestion. Although listed in 1953 as a building of historic interest, it was demolished for road widening in April 1956. The recently-built stores of Marks & Spencer and Woolworth's can be seen just beyond it.

HIGH STREET FROM THE AIR c.1927

This view illustrates the former character of central Staines with its mixture of commercial, industrial and domestic buildings, and open ground south of the High Street in the area now occupied by South Street and the Bus Station. The large complex of buildings housing the Linoleum Factory can be seen in the left foreground where the Two Rivers development is now situated. Elmsleigh House and a range of farm buildings are visible in the right foreground where the Elmsleigh Centre now stands. Beside the railway embankment was 2½ acres of land on which stood an aeroplane hangar 75 ft. square, seen here on the right. This was erected here by Mumford & Lobb in 1926 and used as a repair shop, furniture store, etc. By this time the railway bridge had been rebuilt in its present form, replacing an arched bridge which forced high vehicles into the centre of the road.

HIGH STREET 1945

En route to the muster at the Market Square (page 22), the inhabitants of Staines were treated to an impressive march past by numerous Service and voluntary units. The salute was taken outside the Majestic Cinema, where this photograph was taken. Unfortunately, war-time censorship only allowed mention of an army unit and a "tank" among the participants. The model seen dipping its gun barrel to the saluting base is in fact a mark of the Cromwell Tank Cruiser, a Centaur, one of the many types developed at the nearby establishment at Longcross and only used in the U.K. for training. The mobilisation of the "Home Front", undoubtedly a major factor in the victory, was achieved in Staines, as elsewhere. Just visible above in Lewis' upstairs window are his daughter and his granddaughter, now Mrs. Milner. The latter recalls her grandfather's accounts of using German prisoners-of-war during the First World War to cut withies at Eton for use in basket-making.

MARMADUKE'S HOTEL c.1925

Before the building of the Majestic Cinema between the railway bridge and the present Post Office, a large house, originally named Fairfield House, stood here, and the land on which Fairfield Avenue was built was part of the same property. The last people to live here were Dr. De la Motte and his family, who were in residence by 1890. In the early 1920s, however, it was briefly used as a convent school before becoming first a restaurant known as the Silver Teapot and then Marmaduke's Hotel, as shown here. One relic of its earlier days was the splendid catalpa (Indian bean) tree which overhung the pavement in the front garden. This in turn became the Sevens Hotel, owned by Mr. Angelo Clark, who sold it in 1929 and bought a small island near Sark in the Channel Islands. The building was demolished to make way for the Majestic Cinema.

MAJESTIC CINEMA c.1949

The first Staines cinema to offer "talkies" was the Majestic, opened on 11th December, 1929, with a pre-release showing of "The Great Gabbo". This large edifice took only eight months to build, work having started on 19th April. The architect was S.B. Pritlove and the building incorporated a restaurant and dance hall, as well as seating for 1,558 people. The interior, designed by W.E. Greenwood, included columns, towers and other Italianate architectural features under a blue "sky". It was equipped with a five-rank Compton organ. In 1932 it was leased by the owners, Majestic Theatres Corporation, to County Cinemas, and passed with that circuit to Odeon in 1939. The Ealing comedy, "Kind Hearts and Coronets", showing at the time of the photograph, was released in 1949 and starred Dennis Price and Alec Guinness. The cinema closed on 27th May, 1961, and was replaced by the present Majestic House.

HIGH STREET LOOKING WEST 1956

In December 1921 the local electricity company had installed temporary electric arc lamps suspended over the middle of the High Street during the Christmas shopping period. The Chamber of Commerce was enthusiastic, but after enquiring into the cost the Council took no action. The Brentford Gas Company responded by installing improved burners in the gas lamps free of charge, but these were soon superseded by arc lamps. The standards shown here were erected in the 1930s. Kay's Cycle dealership and the electrical engineers V. & D. Keale also dated to the 1930s, while E. & G. Gomm, corn, coal and seed merchants, took over an earlier business here in 1910 and traded from the same building until 1961. Their original distinctive façade had by this time been remodelled, but the firm now boasted a coat of arms denoting a Royal Appointment. On the left, Maxwell & Sons had succeeded Fitzsimmons Bros. in their music warehouse during the 1930s, and G. Laslett, draper, was trading before 1930.

LONDON ROAD c.1908

A quiet traffic-free London Road junction belies the character of what must always have been a busy thoroughfare. The recently completed tarring of the road surface, itself a reaction to the inexorable increase in motor traffic, still reveals evidence of extensive use of horses: however, the new transport technology soon had its own network of dedicated facilities. Staines Motor Works had established itself here c.1905 and prominently displayed its services to the local and passing trade. Its contemporary advertising advised that it had the only fully equipped repair shop and garage in a ten mile radius. The London Road frontage of their works, no. 1 London Road, adjacent to Swinburne Lane, was reputedly once the "Bow Street Runners" station. This strategic position allowed the precursors of the Metropolitan Police to control one of Middlesex's main roads and is also recorded as having lock-up facilities.

STAINES 1961

Aerial views provide a highly informative overview of the development of many parts of the country. This shot of 1961, probably taken in connection with the development of the Staines By-pass, is typical of their value. Of particular note is the loss of many large concerns, clearly seen here, which once employed many thousands. In the middle distance can be seen the Manor Place works of W.E. Sykes, machine tool makers, (see page 53). Also gone in the London Road, running east-west in the foreground, are the bus garage and the premises of Stewart & Ardern, who were Morris agents and dealers at Morris House, no. 37-47. The traffic seen queuing in London Road and Kingston Road is indicative of the extreme impact on the town of the inexorable rise in road use and of the need for a by-pass for the town. In 1959 the Ministry of Transport estimated that over 50% of the local traffic was through traffic and that a by -pass would cut it by half.

41

LONDON ROAD 1947

The last vestiges of the 1947 flood which had so badly affected the area are still visible here, although photographs taken at its height show impassable pavements and deep water across the roadway. Contemporary reports also speak of the flooding being so deep as to necessitate the use of punts to exit the houses here. Some indication of the relative importance of the Staines Garage can be gauged by the number of vehicles it housed to cover timetabled and regular work. In 1938 it was allocated seven buses and 13 coaches. By 1969 this had risen to eight buses and 10 coaches, and in 1981 it had capacity for 10 buses and 17 coaches. The decline in passenger traffic and deregulation led to its closure and demolition in 1996. The telegraph-pole-like feature on the right-hand pavement is thought to be part of the fire alarm system linked to the Fire Station at Market Square. Obscured by the pedestrian is a cast-iron pillar with a push-button which could be used to summon assistance to the scene. This dedicated system, originally patented by William Blenheim of Egham, was reputedly installed in the town by Victor Badois of Thames Street.

ST. MARY'S HALL/NATIONAL BOYS' SCHOOL c.1980

"The National Society for Promoting the Education of the Poor in the Principles of the Established Church" was founded in 1811 with the intention of making the national religion the foundation of national education. Staines has a long history of educational provision supported by various Christian denominations and the London Road premises seem to have been in use as both a chapel and school by 1863. The gabled building with its stone-dressed features consisted of a hall 60 ft. x 25 ft. and one classroom 25 ft. x 12 ft. This accommodated 250 boys taught by a Master in Charge who also undertook religious education. It is reported that London Road itself was used as the playground! Following various late 19th century Education Acts, the Staines National Schools, run by the Local Board since 1885, closed in 1903. The building reverted to the use of the Anglican Parish and was put to various uses including serving as a British Restaurant during the Second World War and later as a dress factory.

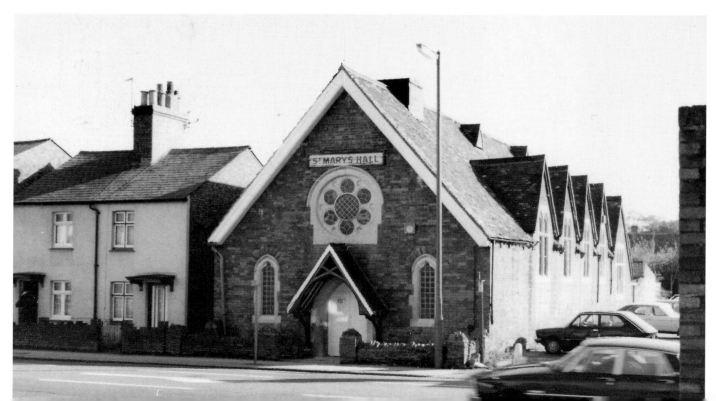

CROOKED BILLET c.1880

Although there seem to have been licensed premises here since at least 1792, the present structure is late Victorian and rebuilt slightly to the east of that shown. As seen here, the original buildings exhibit many interesting architectural features, with two distinct phases of building evident which may both be of 18th century date. At the time of this photograph the landlord was Henry Lord, licensee between 1871 and 1882. The origin of the house's name is open to much speculation, and there are many suggestions as to its original significance: travellers on the main road, however, would have associated it with a particular point on their journey to and from London, as indicated by the milestone set against its face. Examples of these still exist on the A30 and date from the time when it was maintained as a turnpike or privatised road by a trust first established in 1727 to maintain the road from Hounslow to Basingstoke. A tollhouse stood on the south side of the London Road just east of Shortwood Common.

STAINES BY-PASS November 1964

The chronic traffic congestion in Staines was somewhat eased in November 1961 when the two-mile first stage of the Staines By-pass opened, diverting much of the through traffic around the north of the town. Vehicles travelling on the A308, however, still had to pass through the town centre. This problem was rectified when the one-and-a-half-mile-long second stage from the Crooked Billet to Ford Bridge, Ashford, opened on 10th July, 1964, three months ahead of schedule. Some anxiety was expressed about the safety of pedestrians attempting to cross the new road near the Crooked Billet roundabout and an underpass was called for. The River Ash, which passes through a culvert under the road at this point, made that solution impossible, but by the end of November this prefabricated steel footbridge with ramps had been completed. A workman can be seen here putting the finishing touches to the bridge. The Crooked Billet itself is visible underneath the centre of the bridge.

MIDDLESEX & SURREY LAUNDRIES c.1910

This building, still standing at 191-193 London Road, is one of the earliest purpose-built laundries, dating to the late 19th century. It was bought in 1901 by Mr. D.T. Newbegin who built up the business, reaching its peak between the two World Wars. At that time the laundry employed some 500 staff. The work was hot and very labour-intensive. Fabrics were all made from natural fibres which needed ironing – a chore carried out by 100 hand-ironers such as those shown, working from 8 a.m. to 6 p.m. An élite group of the best ironers were responsible for the most delicate items. Their number dwindled with increasing mechanisation and new fabrics until by 1976 only four remained. Water was obtained from artesian wells on the premises. By 1951 there were 20,000 customers and the service was expanded to include dry cleaning. The business remained in the Newbegin family until its closure in March 1976, by which time only about 120 staff remained.

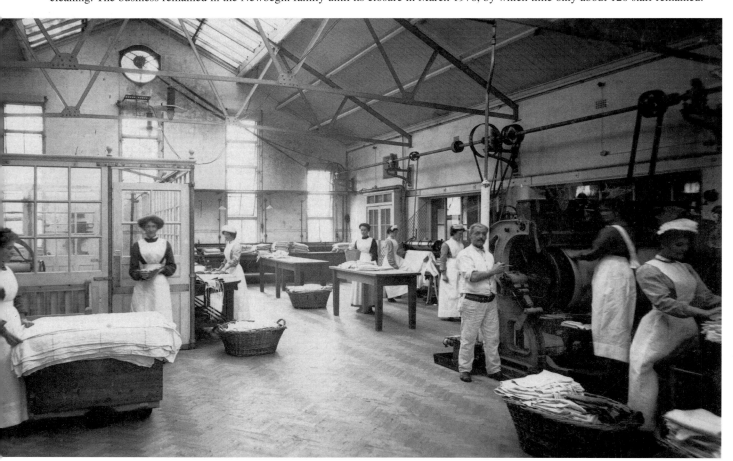

SIDNEY ROAD c.1905

Probably laid out soon after 1890, Sidney Road was developed as a residential street during the following decade, the greater part of the road being built up by 1895, but with the eastern end still running through open land. Greenlands Road and Rosefield Road had also been laid out by that date, but were almost totally devoid of houses. In 1896 Frank Lewis, the basket-maker, moved into Sidney Road and initially ran his business from his home. As shown in the photograph, the street was planted with an avenue of trees to create a pleasant environment for the residents. Although still quite small at the time of the photograph, by November 1933 these had reached such a size that the Council resolved to remove alternate trees to improve the street.

KINGSTON ROAD c.1928

This aerial view gives a clear overall view of this end of Kingston Road, setting some of the other photographs reproduced here in their original context. In London Road in the left-hand corner is the old Police Station, currently (1999) vacant. Behind it is the row of shops called The Broadway. Between London Road and Sidney Road are Stansfeld's brewery depot, Fear Brothers coal and corn merchant's and removal business, the Co-op and the Methodist Church. On the near side of the road, a new parade of shops has replaced the candle factory on the corner of the High Street, destroyed in a spectacular fire in April 1924. In the centre foreground is George Street, with the Kingston Road Schools to its right. Note the flag-pole in the playground, where children would salute the flag on Empire Day. Next to the school is one of the malt houses of the former Knowle Green Brewery, which survives as part of the adult education centre.

KINGSTON ROAD c.1910

Stansfeld & Co, brewers and wine and spirit merchants, maintained an extensive network of depots to the south and west of London for their products. The Swan Brewery at Fulham not only supplied alcoholic refreshment but also offered various types of "mineral" water to their customers. In fact, Staines has a long history of manufacture of carbonated drinks, the firm of H. Taylor at 231, London Road, celebrating their 150th anniversary this year (1999). Other makers in the town included the brewers, Ashby's and Harris. As with many other retailers at the turn of the century, a home delivery service was the norm and by 1892 Stansfeld's were advertising daily delivery within 10 miles of Staines. Another local manufacturer was Alfred Harwood of Thames Street, who in 1908 was charging 1s. 6d. (7½ p) per dozen for syphons of soda water and 5d (2p) per dozen for large bottles. The bottles seem to have been worth more than the contents: a deposit on each hopefully ensured their return.

GEORGE STREET 1974

George Street seems to have been laid out c.1880 in an area still shown as fields on maps of the 1870s. It is possible that it was built as workmen's cottages for the labour force of the adjacent Knowle Green Brewery or the candle factory on the corner of High Street and Kingston Road, which stretched back as far as George Street. Although principally a residential street, by 1886 there were already four tradespeople listed here, of whom two, a confectioner and a tobacconist, would have had shops. There was also a dressmaker, Mrs. Clarke, who may well have been working to supplement her husband's wages, and a chimney sweep, George Stent, who traded from here from about 1881 to at least 1913. A more romantic, if possibly short-lived, business was the Lava roller-skating rink (later Crimble's workshop), advertised in the "Middlesex Chronicle" in 1911 and apparently situated at the junction of George Street and Station Path.

CO-OP, KINGSTON ROAD c.1907

Another familiar delivery vehicle at this time belonged to the Co-operative Society branch in Kingston Road, opened in the 1890s on the site later occupied by Johnson & Clark. When it caught fire on 1st January, 1908, it was considered "one of the most commodious establishments in the town,...well stocked with all kinds of provisions and large assortment of other goods..." The building was restored and by 1914 the Society had 1,400 members and in March opened a new building adjoining, which included a new grocery shop, a cellar, drapery shop with warehouse and a large assembly hall above capable of holding 250-300 people. At the opening ceremony J.E. Johns, one of the Directors, boasted that "The bulk of the goods sold in the Society's shops were supplied by the Society...and they were made under fair conditions of hours, wages and health, and not by sweated labour." They aimed to provide a centre for the education and improvement of the working people of the town.

KINGSTON ROAD 1954

A Green Line coach, stopped en route to its final destination of Gravesend, Kent, was recorded for posterity by Alan Cross in October 1954. The Co-operative Society's stores had expanded further by this time and the numerous departments included coal and coke and funerals. The interior had a pneumatic change system of great fascination to one of the authors as a small boy. Staines, in contrast to today's commercial environment, had a variety of public clocks, the Co-op's electric timepiece, a great boon to travellers and other passers-by, having been erected c.1947. The bus awaiting departure is one of the fleet of the RF type introduced for Green Line service in 1951. On July 1st, 1953, the new 725 service from Windsor to Gravesend was inaugurated and by 1954 was running a half-hourly service.

KINGSTON ROAD c.1920

Although there have been many changes in the enterprises carried out in this parade of shops in Kingston Road, the façades of the single-storey premises have remained remarkably unchanged since their construction. At no. 34B were the premises of Frank Arthur Dommett, antique furniture dealer. His stock also seemed to include somewhat more modern items such as the then fashionable gate-leg tables, rugs and ceramics. The shop is now part of the Staines Adult Education Centre, itself housed in the adjacent complex of buildings once part of Harris's Knowle Green Brewery.

SALVATION ARMY BAND 1931

Staines was established as an outpost of the Colnbrook Corps and the Staines Corps officially opened, in the face of sometimes violent opposition, on 21st August, 1890. Mr. W.J. Sanders joined the Salvation Army in 1890 and formed a band of which he was bandmaster until 1929. The following year he set up the Staines United Temperance Band, which evolved into the present Staines Brass Band. His successor, bandmaster Fowler, is shown here in the centre front. In 1931 he was one of those presented with long-service awards by Col. Bernard Booth (son of Col. Bramwell Booth) on a visit to Staines. Other bandsmen shown are Les Johnson, the Denyer brothers, Leslie Prior and the May brothers. The old Methodist Chapel in Kingston Road, vacant since the building of the new church opposite, was purchased and adapted by the Army in 1892. This was used until demolished and replaced by a new, larger hall opened in January 1953. In 1990 this in turn closed when the Woodthorpe Road School site, Ashford, was acquired for the Army's local headquarters.

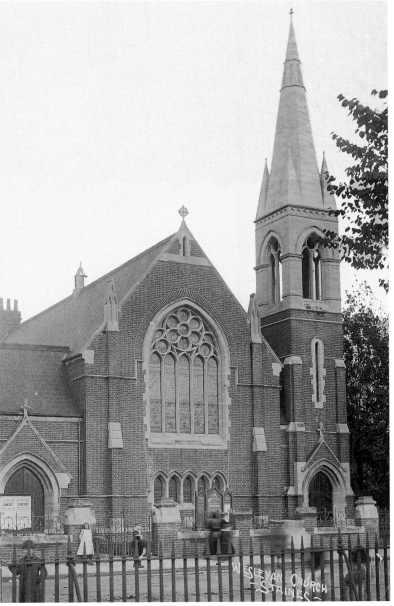

KINGSTON ROAD SCHOOL c.1910

Educational provision for the majority of the children of Staines had been located at a variety of sites in the district. In 1885 a Board of local worthies took over the running of these establishments and continued its rôle until the Middlesex County Council took over responsibility for educational matters and opened this new facility in 1903. Its initial capacity was for 700 children, with separate schools for girls and boys. Its first boys' head teacher was Mark Mullens, known affectionately as "Gaffer", who had previously been in charge of the nearby London Road Board School, which duly closed in 1903. Mr. Mullens (1853-1927) was also a local Councillor for the Hythe Ward of Egham U.D.C. and is commemorated in a street name there. Kingston Road School was initially built to provide education until the then leaving age of 14. New facilities further along Kingston Road were started in 1939, to become the Matthew Arnold Secondary Modern School. The provision of Junior education continued here until 1991 when a new school, Kingscroft County Junior, was opened in Park Avenue.

METHODIST CHURCH 1907

In 1771 John Wesley had visited Staines, preaching in two small converted cottages where he was enthusiastically received. The town did not have a purpose-built chapel until 1853. This stood on the south side of Kingston Road. It was replaced in 1890 by the building shown here, while the old chapel was sold to the Salvation Army. The new Methodist church, situated on the other side of Kingston Road, was of red brick with stone dressings and a spire at the south west corner. At the time this photograph was taken, the local Wesleyans boasted their own brass band, which held concerts at the church together with various local vocalists such as Miss B. Avis, Miss Jessie Avis, Miss Ethel Saul and Mr. F. Hollis Harvey. The newly-formed Staines Temperance Band, which was yet to make a public appearance, held a New Year party in the Wesleyan Hall in 1931. In 1987 this building was replaced with the present commodious modern building off Thames Street.

STAINES JUNCTION c.1920

Many fine railway photographs are taken from the convenient vantage point of a footbridge linking station platforms and this view looking west is no exception. Approaching on the Reading line is a Class M7 0-4-4T tank locomotive, no. 32. This was the largest, most powerful, and most numerous L.S.W.R. engine of this wheel arrangement. It was the first design of the Locomotive Superintendent of the L.S.W.R., Dougald Drummond, and was introduced in 1897. The Staines Junction designation related to the added importance gained by the town's position as a link between the line to Windsor and that to Reading, both serving London's Waterloo terminus. The Windsor line, authorised in 1847 at the height of the railway boom, reached Staines in 1848 and was followed in 1856 by the line to Wokingham and Reading. Staines, now being only 30 minutes' travelling time from London, greatly benefited from a tourist trade based on the Thames and surrounding attractions.

STATION BOOKSTALL 1947

As well as acting as a focus for passenger and freight traffic, the new railway network supported ancillary traders providing refreshment and other facilities. Originally employing a fleet of horse and carts to distribute daily newspapers and periodicals, W.H. Smith opened their first railway bookstall at Euston Station in 1848, and at one time had over 1,000 such outlets. These sites offered a convenient service for the new daily commuters and other travellers at a time when the railways were the principal mode of transport for long journeys and many short ones. The bookstall at Staines Junction was opened before 1862 and the fixture shown here was installed in 1920 to replace an earlier structure. On 4th December of that year, the "Middlesex Chronicle" reported that Mr. Harvey, of the Staines bookstall, and Mr. Phillimore, of the Egham bookstall, had recently attended the firm's centenary dinner at the Holborn Restaurant for 923 Smith's staff with over 21 years' service. The bookstall continued trading until 1974.

LEACROFT 1904

Flooding was a not infrequent problem in Staines, which lies at the junction of several tributaries to the Thames. The River Ash was one of those which burst its banks in 1904 and Leacroft was naturally badly affected. Ever resourceful, local people could find a solution to most problems and the local postman can be seen on the nearer punt making his deliveries by water. On the left is the Old Red Lion, a hostelry believed to have its origins in the 17th century, although this has yet to be demonstrated with certainty. The bar at that time was just a small room with a counter across which the landlord, George Jeffery, would serve his beer from barrels standing nearby, and also sold sweets to the local children. Facing the camera in the centre is the building which was used as a skittle alley for the Old Red Lion and later as a workshop for the smithy adjoining the pub. Quoits were also played here on the green.

STAINES VOLUNTEERS c.1904

The men of H (Staines) Company, 2nd (later 8th) Volunteer Battalion, Middlesex Regiment, are pictured here on parade, possibly at the opening of their drill hall at Leacroft in November 1904. The new building was of Fletton brick, the front being faced with red brick and rough-cast. It contained a 90 ft. x 45 ft. drill hall, recreation room, armoury and officers' rooms, with the Sergeant Instructor's quarters above. Col. Bott took the chair at the opening ceremony. Prior to this, the Company had no permanent home, and for some while had met in an old barn in London Road until 1903, when Messrs. Ashby let them use the tun-room at the Knowle Green Brewery. Their enthusiasm was apparently unaffected, as in December 1899, 40 men from the Staines Company applied to join the Corps of Imperial Volunteers then being formed for active service in South Africa. Six were finally selected and given a good "send-off" at a smoking concert.

RAIL CRASH, 9th August, 1957

Many residents recall this occasion when an eight-coach electric train, unit no. 5225, drew away from the up platform with the signal at danger and collided with a class 700 steam engine, no.30688, used in shunting, as it crossed from the east yard to the down line. The collision occurred just below the Knowle Green railway bridge. Both lines were closed for some hours, with buses laid on to ferry passengers between Ashford and Egham. The steam engine was turned on its side and the front of the first coach of the passenger train, including the motorman's cab, ripped open. Miraculously, no-one was killed, although 14 were injured, of whom five were detained in hospital, including the driver and fireman of the steam engine and the motorman of the electric train. Some employees of T.G. Simmons & Son, of Leacroft, were among the first on the scene and rescued the crewmen and some passengers. Traffic on Kingston Road was held up for some time by a fire engine hosing down the wreckage from the bridge.

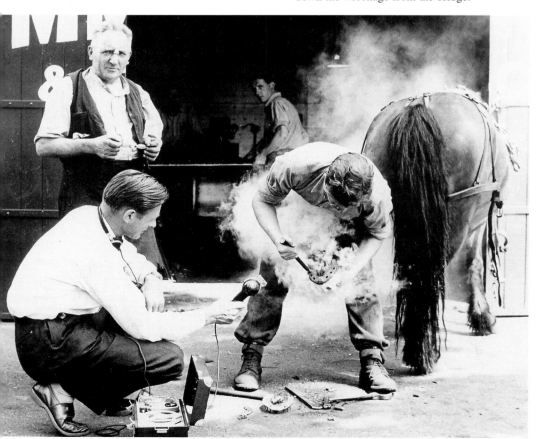

SIMMONS' SMITHY c.1957

Mr. Tom Simmons came to Staines in 1910 and bought a forge situated next to the Red Lion at Leacroft and formerly used by Mr. Lucas for shoeing horses. Mr. Simmons developed this into a more general smithy and wheelwright's shop. He soon established a reputation for building high-quality horse-drawn vehicles for local firms. In 1922, after an apprenticeship as an engineer, his son, Rodney, joined the business and the old skittle alley adjacent to the forge was demolished to make way for a vehicle body-building and repairs shop. The following year, a paint shop was added. In 1932 a nearby site was purchased, facing Leacroft Green. Most of the existing buildings were demolished and rebuilt over the following years, replacing the earlier Simmons premises. By 1960 the new buildings housed a flourishing motor body-building, panel-beating and welding business. Tom Simmons died in April 1959, aged 82. In 1968 the firm was taken over by Crimbles. The photograph shows a BBC sound engineer recording a horse being shod, for the BBC Sound Archive.

SYKES FOOTBALL TEAM 1950-51

Famed throughout the world for their gear-cutting technology, the firm of W.E. Sykes established its first workshop at Egham Hythe in 1927. Originally, the company specialised in gear-shaper cutters, but by 1935 the Manor Works at Staines had been built and tooled up for the production of gear-generating machines. Products were exported from here world-wide even before the last war and Staines products were soon seen as the industry standard. In 1951 the local press recorded that the Manor Works were capable of producing machines for the production of gears from 5' 6" to ¹⁄₁₀" diameter. In the same year the 500,000th gear-shaper cutter was produced. The five acre works at Staines had a payroll at the time of nearly 1,000 and, as well as the usual social facilities associated with large companies, the firm had its own sports ground and ran a team in the newly-formed Staines District League. W.E. Sykes were later taken over by the 600 Group, the company moved away and the site was sold for housing in 1986.

COUNCIL OFFICES c.1972

During the 1920s Staines Urban District Council had outgrown the Town Hall. In October 1931 it was proposed to purchase part of the Staines Brewery estate for a car park and convert the brewery stables into council offices. Cllr. Low commented that, in time, "Staines would be a borough and would want appropriate and dignified offices and not converted stables." The scheme was still under discussion in May 1936, when the lease on their premises at 33, Clarence Street was soon to run out. The Clarence Street offices were eventually given up in 1952, when the Clerk's Department moved to London Road. By 1970, the Council had offices scattered around Staines and new premises were desperately needed. The construction of this building was commenced and it was finally opened by John Pett, Chairman of the Council, in September 1972. Costing £400,000, the building was the first of a planned complex of civic facilities at Knowle Green. Cllr. Pett considered it "a building which represents the skills and arts of craftsmen". It was extended in 1985.

KINGSTON ROAD c.1933

These brand new shopping facilities at Kingston Road, complemented by those at the Broadway and Stainash Parade (built 1933-4) no doubt provided an important incentive to shop locally for the residents of the estates springing up to the south and east of Staines. The six shops at 139-149 were erected where meadows and cottages once stood. They included at least two concerns already established in the area and at 139, out of shot at the end of the parade, was R.T. Jubb's butcher's, which opened to a massive campaign in the local press, advising new customers that his prices would always be the lowest in Middlesex! At no. 145, the Staines and District Co-operative Society had opened a branch to its headquarters at the other end of Kingston Road.

FLOODS, KINGSTON ROAD, 1947

1947 has been called a year of weather records, both nationally and locally. The frost and snow of the first months of the year were followed by a sudden thaw which overwhelmed the area's river system, causing widespread flooding worse than any since 1894. Rainfall in March, at about 4¾ ins., was the heaviest for over 100 years. One of the worst-hit areas in Staines was the residential estate around Kingston Road, where the water was several feet deep. The photograph shows the road outside Job's Dairy at 147, Kingston Road. The cost of the damage in Staines was estimated at about £10,000 and, as elsewhere, a flood relief fund was set up to help those affected. In contrast, May was the warmest for over a century and at the end of May the temperature locally exceeded 83°F for five consecutive days. August was the hottest, driest and sunniest since 1881, with a drought lasting 37 days, and rainfall from the end of July to December was the lowest on record.

FENTON AVENUE AND STRODE'S CRESCENT c.1933

Staines shared in the tremendous inter-war boom in house-building. Up and down the country, estates large and small were erected in short order to meet the desire for affordable home ownership. The Victoria Park Estate off the Kingston Road was one such development and was the work of the firm of F. Taylor Junior & Co. Contemporary reports provide interesting detail of the scheme and the popularity of such developments at the time when the Depression was at its height. Four types of "Wonder Houses" were on offer at prices ranging from £445 to £566, each with deposits of £25. Taylors also advised prospective owners that each house was built on a bed of solid concrete and that only the best materials were used. By June 1933, of the total estate of 213 houses, 200 had been erected and sold in 12 months. The original estate of 18 acres was broken up into five streets, including Fenton Avenue and Strode's Crescent, where an open space had been preserved for the benefit of tenants on the estate, and grass verges and trees planted.

MATTHEW ARNOLD SCHOOL c.1955

One consequence of the rapidly expanding population of the area was the need to provide school places for local children. Middlesex County Council, as the Education Authority, opted to build a brand new facility on what was literally a "green field" site. The new campus was to be called the Matthew Arnold County Secondary School in honour of the Victorian poet and educationalist, Matthew Arnold (1822-1888). Building commenced in 1939 but was unfinished when war broke out. Senior pupils from the bomb-damaged Kingston Road School were transferred here and at the end of hostilities an urgent effort was made to complete the work in order to provide the further accommodation required as a result of the raising of the school leaving age under the Education Act of 1944. Separate provision was made for 960 boys and girls, with the post-war work carried out to the same design and materials to preserve the character of the school. Expenditure of £147,760 was authorised and the work completed in 1954.

COTTAGE HOSPITAL c.1920

In March 1908, the Staines, Feltham and Sunbury U.D.Cs. and the Rural District united to form the Staines Joint Hospital Board, which first met in February 1910. The resulting hospital was opened by Lady Clarke on 9th May, 1914, thanks to a legacy of £2,000 from Mrs. James Harris. The golden key used in the ceremony was made by B.L. Virgo, jeweller, of High Street. The architect, Mr. Leslie T. Moore, A.R.I.B.A., designed a building with single-storey wards to protect patients from noise overhead and arranged in a "Y" shape so that convalescents could lie out of doors in a sheltered position. The floors were covered with linoleum donated by the Staines Linoleum Company. Miss Bramwell was appointed as Matron and Miss Clifford as Staff Nurse. The opening of Ashford Hospital in 1939 diminished the rôle of the Cottage Hospital and it closed in the early 1980s and was demolished in autumn 1986.

TEMPLEDENE AVENUE c.1934

The shortage of housing in the period after the First World War led to the building of numerous council and private housing estates around the 1930s. Jubb & Ball had begun their building activities in Staines with the Laleham House Estate c.1929. This view of Templedene Avenue was taken when the street was nearing completion. By 10th August, 1934, the "Staines & Egham News" announced that this "most attractive development scheme" was completed and all but one of the houses sold. In October, Staines U.D.C. agreed to take over the five electric street lamps in the road, but declined responsibility for the two gas lamps at the entrance to the Avenue, which were said to be for display lighting only. Since March 1934, Mr. Jubb had been planning his next scheme, which was for the adjacent eight-acre Pavilion Gardens Estate: an ambitious project with houses facing inwards across two carriageways to a central area comprising recreation grounds, a tea garden, tennis courts, putting green and a pavilion with billiard room and a hall. Mr. Jubb formed a residents' club which met here, renting the premises from him for £10 per week, with £12 for rates and insurance. All the houses were semi-detached, with gas and electricity in every room and coal hearths in the four principal rooms. Prices ranged from £595 to £795. The deposit required for homes there was higher than in Templedene Avenue – £15-£25 according to the style of house. The central gardens have now long vanished under houses built since the War.

PENTON HOOK LOCK HOUSE 1909

The imposing stuccoed lock house was built in 1814 to provide accommodation for the keeper of the new Thames lock. Recorded wages for the post, although apparently low during the 19th century, would be supplemented by maintained accommodation as a perquisite of the job. As well as requiring a lock keeper's attention to the needs of passing traffic, the increasing popularity of the river for leisure purposes brought others to this attractive spot. In June 1852 it was recorded that the "idle and disorderly of Staines and Laleham" were frequenting the lock island on Sundays and a warning notice to trespassers was erected. Samuel Myhill, seen here with his family, had originally been in charge of the lock at Hambledon and retired in 1913.

PENTON HOOK c.1930

More evidence of the rôle of Staines as a resort town in the early decades of this century is provided by the facilities available to tourists. Angling was also an attraction and in 1880 Penton Hook was described as "a perfect trout preserve". In 1906 the Penton Hall Hotel near Penton Hook advertised tennis, boating and fishing facilities and stabling and motor accommodation. It was also a temperance establishment at a time when the movement was at its peak and resorts routinely catered for the non-imbiber. The Avenue Hotel, Thameside, had been opened c.1914 by Thomas Grimmett to cater specifically for this market. As well as providing accommodation for guests, it catered for day trippers attracted to the Thames and the passing delights of the traffic using Penton Hook Lock. Its proximity to the busy but dangerous environs of the river is illustrated by the notice advertising the availability of rescue equipment in the event of need.

HOSPITAL SUNDAY PARADE c.1914

The bequest which facilitated the building of the Cottage Hospital in 1914 had not removed the necessity for fund-raising, although Staines Urban District Council guaranteed any deficit on the running costs for three years. Fund-raising events included a "Pound Day" on the anniversary of the opening, when local people donated £1 or equivalent goods. An annual church parade was instituted by the Amalgamated Friendly Societies. According to the "Middlesex Chronicle" in 1915, a flag day and house-to-house collections on the previous day, together with a concert by the Town Band, preceded the main event. The procession, headed in 1915 by the Ancient Order of Foresters with their banner, set off from the Great Western Railway Station in Moor Lane and marched through the main streets to St. Peter's Church, where a service was held and £1 15s. 6d. collected during the service. The photograph shows members of the Town Band and the Manchester Unity of Oddfellows in Gresham Road and behind them the Staines or Egham Fire Brigade, both of whom participated.

BEACH'S GARAGE c.1965

Harry Beach established his taxi and coach firm at this garage at 12, Gresham Road, adjacent to his home, in the 1920s. While many bus and coach operators running scheduled services were taken over by London Transport in 1933, a considerable number of small, independent operators continued to offer vehicles for hire. This concern was well-known locally and at its peak boasted a fleet of 17 coaches. As well as providing transport for excursions by local schools, firms and social organisations, Beach's Luxury Coaches offered regular outings for local people, who could book seats through Kennards and selected shops in neighbouring towns, who acted as booking agents. In August 1949 they were advertising daily runs (excluding Sundays) to Brighton, Southsea (for the Isle of Wight), Bognor and Littlehampton, besides less frequent trips to other resorts and to Whipsnade Zoo. The firm closed down in the late 1970s, but the garage shown here stood until recently, latterly occupied by Whyte's Airport Services Ltd.

ST. PETER'S CHURCH c.1904

In response to the rising population, in 1874 the Vicar, the Rev. Canon Furse, instigated the erection of a small brick building in Wyatt Road known as St. Peter's Mission Chapel. This was replaced by a larger iron building in Edgell Road in 1885. In 1890 Sir Edward Clarke, Q.C., the Solicitor-General, purchased "Thorncote" (later renamed Jamnagar House) and he and his wife began to attend the mission church. They proved generous benefactors to the church and Sir Edward purchased a nearby field where Lady Kathleen Clarke laid the foundation stone for the new church on 22nd July, 1893. The building was designed by G.H. Fellowes Prynne and built by Messrs. Goddard and Sons of Farnham, with Mr. W. Augur of Staines as Clerk of Works. The total cost was nearly £10,000. The building was consecrated by the Right Rev. Lord Bishop of Marlborough on Saturday, 28th July, 1894. Two years later Sir Edward decided to add an organ at a cost of over £1,000.

RICHMOND ROAD c.1920

This photograph, by Thomas Leonard Gadd, of the Gresham Studio, Chertsey, captures the character of this quiet residential street. A map of 1866 shows that Gresham Road had only eight semi-detached houses on its north side and open fields stretched from there to the railway line. Richmond Road seems to have been developed c.1880, and by 1882, W. Bates had opened a grocer's shop here. This was probably the same shop shown here at no. 8, run in 1921 by Francis H. Choakes. A directory of 1914 indicates that light industry had gained a foothold in the street in the shape of the Juno Manufacturing Co. Ltd., metal stampers, but they had gone by this time, perhaps a victim of the First World War

JUBILEE GARDENS c.1904

The Diamond Jubilee of Queen Victoria's accession on 22nd June, 1897, was enthusiastically celebrated throughout the country. In Staines, "the town was decorated both elegantly and lavishly, and its illumination by night was very fine". A dinner for adults was served at noon at the Town Hall and "a commodious room opposite" and consisted of roast beef, plum pudding, beer, etc. Later, the children were entertained to tea. Sports were held and "in the evening the illuminations on the river side formed a striking spectacle." As a permanent memorial of the occasion, Holgate's Wharf was purchased and laid out the following year as a public garden, the cost being met by public subscription. The gardens along the riverbank have been a popular leisure area ever since, as seen here. On the corner of Laleham Road and Prospect Place is the dairy and post office run by Mason Davey. The present public promenade from the gardens to the Lammas was planned by the Council in 1947.

THAMES STREET 1908

Photographer and publisher Leonard Caspell, recorder of this and many other local scenes, was resident at 3, Thames Street, where he also traded as a picture-frame maker and was Deputy Registrar of Marriages for the area. He recorded this watery view in April 1908 when the heightened river overflowed its by now well-defined banks. Such scenes, once commonplace, have become much more of a rarity due both to the improved hydro-engineering of the Thames valley and to the generally decreased flow of the river and its tributaries. Also captured for posterity was the passage of Joseph Samuel Greenwood, a cow-keeper of Edgell Road. In practice, this contemporary description usually meant milk producer and retailer, the single churn and horse and trap delivery being an everyday sight in the area at the turn of the century.

HOOK ON AND SHOOT OFF COTTAGES 1914-18

These cottages, probably dating to the early 19th century, derive their name from the methods used to convey horse-drawn barges across the Thames at this point, where the towpath cross to the other bank. When going upstream, this was a tricky operation involving whipping up the horses to gain maximum momentum before casting off the tow-rope to shoot the barge across the stream. The horses had either to be taken round by Staines Bridge or carried across on the ferry. Outside the nearer cottage is a member of one of the Territorial regiments guarding the vital railway bridge over the Thames. By August 1914, all such bridges were so closely guarded that boats were prohibited from passing under them after dark. In July 1915, at the nearby Pack Horse Hotel, one member of the Staines Railway Bridge Guard, Sergeant Major Banks, of the East Surrey Regiment, was presented with a Warrant Officer's belt by his comrades to mark his promotion.

THAMES STREET c.1950

The colossal changes that have occurred in the town during the past half century are vividly illustrated here. A wide range of specialist shops which once extended to the High Street junction are shown in this photograph and such is the pace of change that the only structure now left intact in this view is the wall of the Pack Horse (now Thames Lodge) car park in the left foreground. The pleasing elevation of Millers Corner at no. 89, with its once-familiar turret echoing that of the Margaret Pope School, was the last retail premises in the parade, which also contained an antique shop and the Spinning Wheel restaurant. Even the adjacent turning off Thames Street, Tothill Street, has now vanished, giving its name to a multi-storey car park. The street was originally named after the eponymous local family of medical practitioners when it was laid out in 1931. The last of the family, Dr. Frederick Charles Tothill, who had been Medical Officer of Health for the town, left Staines in 1921.

FIRE BRIGADE PROCESSION 1906

This unusual view of Thames Street was recorded on Wednesday, 27th June, 1906, when the Staines Fire Brigade christened their new fire engine. Like their first steam fire engine, which they had acquired in 1876, this appliance was made by the well-known firm of Merryweather. A procession was organised, in which 20 engines from neighbouring towns participated, led by one of the local bands. This was followed by a competition in which the Feltham brigade emerged the winners by "throwing the farthest jet". Apart from the spectacular nature of the parade, which was the photographer's raison d'être, his image also helps to record the contemporary street scene. Of particular note is the fact that, at this date, retailing of any sort had not been established beyond the Margaret Pope School, identifiable by its small spire. The arcaded building on the right was part of the Congregational Chapel, or its school rooms erected 1867.

5, THAMES STREET c.1908

No. 5, Thames Street was one of the many little shops which once existed at the northern end of Thames Street, cleared for modern retailing in the form of a department store. A wide range of traders occupied this area. Some, like Mrs. Amelia Clarke, combined their retailing with a craft, in this case dressmaking, which she offered here between c.1895 and c.1914. Her stock, attractive to contemporary eyes, is of especial interest to latter-day collectors of both toys and postcards. In fact, all the postcards on display seem to be of the comic variety, illustrating the Edwardian crazes and concerns. Perhaps this card was produced by her next-door neighbour at no. 7, Leonard Caspell, who was one of Staines' own postcard publishers and was responsible for many cards showing local views and images of special events.

THAMES STREET c.1907

Road works, a familiar sight to modern residents, are not a new phenomenon, although fewer workmen are now employed. This photograph is thought to show gas mains being laid in the spring of 1907, followed by the laying of tarmacadam. Ellis & Co., grocers, had closed by 1914. The row of shops on the left was demolished for road widening in 1954. Swann & Co.'s chemist's shop on the corner (later Waine's china and glass shop) was a well-known landmark, visible from some distance along the High Street. Denyer's cycle shop, on the left, represents Staines' oldest business, Edmund Denyer having been in business as a collar-maker in the High Street by 1798. He was succeeded in the saddlery and rope-making business by Richard and then Edmund J. Denyer, who for a few years also ran the shop seen here. The saddler's shop survived until purchased for road-widening in the early 1930s. Mr. Denyer died in 1936.